Sail, Race and Win

by the same author

Dinghy Team Racing
Start to Win
The Rules Book

Sail, Race and Win

Eric Twiname

NAUTICAL BOOKS
MACMILLAN LONDON

First published in Great Britain 1982 by
NAUTICAL BOOKS
An imprint of Macmillan London Limited
4 Little Essex Street
London WC2R 3LF

Associated companies throughout the world

Printed in Great Britain by
The Pitman Press, Bath

British Library Cataloguing in Publication Data

Twiname, Eric
Sail, race and win.
I. Sailboat racing
II. Title
797.1'4 GV826.5

ISBN 0-333-33174-5

Contents

Editor's note

Eric Twiname wrote three books which have had a major impact on the sailing world. These were *Dinghy Team Racing*, *Start to Win* and *The Rules Book*.

He used to joke with me as his editor that he had only three sailing books in him so the development of *Sail, Race and Win* took us into uncharted – and unexpected – waters.

Eric started the book in 1978, initially as a sequel to *Start to Win*. During the following two years the book went through three drafts at a time when Eric was hampered by illness. The going was not easy but, shortly before he died, the book had evolved to its present shape.

Eric passionately believed that too much emphasis is given today to the technical aspects of racing and that more consideration should be given to the impact of the individual on performance. He developed the concept of self-coaching to show how winning skills could be effectively developed through the learning process. In this book he gave a really practical programme on how to put these ideas into practice.

Sail, Race and Win does not present any easy magical formula for moving you up the fleet. What it does, however, is to highlight the 'people' side of racing and to stimulate self-improvement through an honest appraisal of a neglected aspect of the business.

We hope that Eric would have approved of the final outcome. The third draft required substantial editing, some re-writing and re-ordering of his material. I should like to thank Gill Freeman for her patient work in this area, and Eric's father, mother and brother – Alec, Helen and John – for their support throughout.

This last work is a dedication to Eric Twiname – a unique intelligent sensitive man who has made a major contribution to sailing literature during the last decade.

Oliver Freeman

Photographic acknowledgements and captions are on page 155.

1 Teach yourself to win

Many books have been written on the techniques and tactics of winning races. Books by world champions on how they do it, books by people who can write but can't win and books by people who can neither write nor win. Books by the dozen. The best of them relate in well illustrated detail the practical techniques and strategies you should employ to achieve success on the water. They all tell you that if you really want to win, you can. But, from experience we all know that wanting to win isn't enough. We all want to win, or we wouldn't be racing. So why don't we?

In the first place it's statistically impossible. Not everyone can be a champion or there would be no-one to do the losing. 'All right, given that impossibility,' you might ask, 'if I really study and take to heart everything these champions tell me, why do I still not reach the heights I'd like to and of which I know in myself that I am capable?'

The main reason is that a book can teach us only so much. Ultimately you teach yourself. And if your racing is not as good as you would like and improving only slowly, or not at all, it is because you are failing not so much as a sailor but as a sailing coach.

Race winning seems to easy when the author takes you through the start into clear wind and a good early position, up the first beat (taking care to make a few but unimportant errors), niftily round the first mark so everybody gets out of your way, then down the first reach like a bat out of hell, an effortless and immaculate gybe, a place or two on the second reach by getting everything just so, followed by some flawless shift-work on the next beat to put you in contention for the lead, which you gain just before the finish.

Try it yourself and it just doesn't work out like that. It's not enough to know how others do their winning, though it is obviously some help. You must be able to transform their words into your action. And to do that the job of being your own sailing coach must be taken seriously: you must teach yourself to win. Which is, after all, what the champions themselves have done. No-one taught Elvström to win except Elvström himself.

Becoming your own coach

Other sports take the business of coaching and training very seriously. Yet in sailing, which involves the whole mind and body more than any other sport, serious coaching is confined to teaching youngsters up to a certain level and stops before reaching the level which would benefit most helmsmen. In many countries it begins again with the coaching of potential Olympic talent, but all that most of these schemes have managed to do is to raise the less competent Olympic aspirants to a higher level. Many schemes have actually killed off that essential gold medal-winning edge of individual flair, and have instilled attitudes in the crew which make them vulnerable under the extreme pressure of major events like the Olympic Games.

So you can best start becoming your own coach by looking at what is necessary, not what already exists. If you are to do a good job of teaching yourself you should begin by understanding the role you must play in this game of self-teaching, since the job of coach is different from that of the sailor.

The sailor wants to get out there and sail better and faster than anyone else. It is the coach's job to help him do this, but the coach's real interest is in long-term progress – and that may mean viewing things quite differently from his pupil. It is this difference of viewpoint that produces results in sailing, stopping you from getting stuck at one level, and moving you to develop your sailing abilities and find greater enjoyment.

The sailor and coach, for example, have different reactions to mistakes that happen during a race. For the helmsman who makes them they are frustrating and annoying obstacles which cost him places and prevent his doing better. For the coach, mistakes are welcomed as imperfections in sailing ability which he can help the sailor work on and iron out, so they will not recur in future races.

The coach is the thinker, the analyst, the objective observer. The sailor is the doer. The sailor cannot improve without this element of self-teaching. The quality and degree of self-teaching determines how close the sailing self will come to fulfilling all the natural abilities which are inherently there, but which must be brought out by the coaching self.

This necessarily means a more thoughtful and analytical way of tackling racing than most people are used to. Yet it is exactly through such an approach that the champions have become champions. We can see well enough how superbly and flawlessly they sail their races, but that perfection in their external performance has developed from the inner self – which makes their minds work in the right way.

In the 1974 Laser World Championships in Bermuda a young helmsman called John Bertrand finished 39th. He'd expected to do better, and next time he did: he won almost every race, to take the championship by a huge margin. Afterwards he was asked what he did that made such a tremendous difference to his sailing. 'I stopped sailing for six months and just thought about it' he replied. 'That was the most valuable six months of the lot.' Just to prove it was no fluke he went on to win the Laser Worlds again and the Finn Gold Cup at the first attempt.

Priorities

What most helmsmen are looking for is some way of improving as quickly as they reasonably can with the minimum of effort. Everyone is different and the areas of their sailing that need to be worked on are also different. Even two people of equal standard racing the same class are bound to have different strengths and weaknesses, though overall these balance out so the two sailors are competitive with one-another. But when we look at two people of very different standards, the differences are enormous.

The skills that someone at the middle or back of the fleet needs to work on for improvement are totally different from those refinements of technique, attitude and boat tune which would boost the club champion's performance. And what may be crucial to the Olympic aspirant will make little or no difference to the placing of a club tail-ender.

A top flight helmsman, for example, may go through half a dozen centreboards until he has satisfied himself that the hydrodynamic shapes of the leading and trailing edges are the best possible. In a quarter of an hour's racing the best board might give him three lengths over the worst. But the tail-ender might lose that distance in just ten seconds by being overpowered in a gust or by bearing too far off the wind through losing concentration for a few seconds. Any time and effort spent by the middle or back-of-the-fleet man on attempting to acquire this perfect centreboard shape would be a total waste. The gains, even if he made his centreboard perfect, would be far too small to make any difference to his performance. A little time, on the other hand, spent in sharpening his concentration, improving his handling of gusts, or thoroughly getting the hang of windshifts would make a tremendous difference to his finishing positions.

So the first thing you must do is put on your coaching hat and do what John Bertrand did: turn to the most powerful weapon available – thought. And the first stage of thinking must be to assess, as objectively as possible, the present state of your sailing, its strengths and weaknesses. The purpose of this assessment is to pinpoint priorities. Emphasis can then be given to those things at which you are weakest and therefore will provide the biggest gains for the least effort. This is how you use the idea of being your own coach and so getting a different viewpoint from usual.

The reason you are weakest in certain areas is most likely because you don't like them. Light air experts tend to dislike heavy weather and *vice versa*. Boat speed merchants tend not to like shifting winds, shy starters tend to dislike the start and so on. By taking a more objective, coach-like point of view it becomes easier to look analytically at the whole of your performance. Right now you are not worrying about how to put anything right, only looking for what is not as good as it could be.

At this stage, the more problems that can be identified the better – the biggest barrier to most helmsmen's improvement is their blindness to their own shortcomings.

Once this assessment has been completed, the coach-self can work out how to teach the sailing-self the necessary refinements of technique, boat tune or mental attitudes which will make the desired improvement in overall performance. Goals can be set, and if you are someone who works well to a system, you can prepare a programme for yourself, much as any coach would for his pupil.

If you are not too keen on routines, the whole process can work more flexibly and spontaneously. Either way it will work, just so long as the coaching-self makes a good job of the initial assessment, works out how to teach the sailing-self what it needs to know and then oversees the whole learning process so the sailing-self really does get the message. From time to time re-assessment will be necessary and a new set of problems will come up as the old ones are resolved.

That is the process which can be set going within yourself and which produces the greatest progress for a given amount of time and effort spent in trying to improve. It is also the process which this book has been written to help with, whatever level a helmsman's sailing ability and whatever kind of boat or board he sails.

2 The secrets of losing

There are two ways of looking at winning. The first is to see it as something magical and mysterious which only the unusually gifted are ever able to do. The second is to see it as the result of a concerted effort given to avoiding losing. The first is superstitious nonsense; the second gives a sensible and very practical way for anyone who really wants to win.

If you are to avoid losing it would be a great help to know why people do lose. Study that and you can learn what stops people winning. Remove those obstacles and you automatically win. Easily enough said, but nothing like so easy to do, and most people studiously avoid looking at why they lose. Instead they become 'blamers', always able to produce the best reasons in the world for their failure to do well. The most popular targets for blame are:

The crew Normally responsible for all bad tacks and, according to the helmsman, any bad tactical moves (the good moves of course have nothing to do with the crew).

The wind Nothing receives more blame for lost races than the wind and, like the crew, it is given very little thanks for the successful results, since these are due entirely to the helmsman's superb skill and judgement.

The sails The wrong sails for prevailing conditions is an old favourite and can always be used when a helmsman has more than one suit from which to choose. An experienced blamer will always have three or more of each sail at his disposal so that this losing reason is always available, except on the occasions on which he wins. A new suit of sails on order is most useful here: 'that won't happen when I get my new suit of North/Sea-horse/Cheret etc.' Sometimes the new suit is on order for an amazingly long time.

The boat Equipment failure provides a field day for the blamer. ('The jib halyard tensioner went on the first beat raking the mast back something horrible. Killed the jib, ruined the slot and brought on enough weather helm to pull a muscle in a weaker man.') A broken item that can be detached from the boat is even better as he can wander about afterwards displaying fragments of block, sheared tiller extension or severed trapeze wire as evidence of misfortune. Weed attached to the centreplate or keel, although popular, is unconvincing unless it can be produced.

Luck Bad luck is our blamer's most consistent ally in explaining away lost races. He is, for some mysterious reason, the object of consistently bad luck in the races he loses, with exact details of which he will regale people given half a chance, or sometimes given no chance at all, such is his need to broadcast the personal injustices he suffers on the water.

The race committee Poorly set courses, start lines or some fault in the starting arrangements: never *quite* bad enough to call for a protest, but unquestionably the reason he lost, as everyone is told afterwards.

Another competitor Some particularly nasty thing another competitor did to him, usually on the start line or first beat. Or even, in advanced cases of blamery, an unspoken conspiracy by the whole fleet to tack on his wind and force him about at every opportunity.

And so on. The reasons – some might say excuses – depend on the experience, frustration and creative ability of the individual. Not only have you all seen these symptoms in your fellow sailors but, if you dare to admit it, you have seen some of them in yourself, since every racing helmsman has at some time found it more comfortable to explain a poor performance by finding external reasons than to accept the real source of the problem – himself. Everyone makes mistakes and the further down the fleet a crew are the more things they are doing wrong – which is exactly why they're further down the fleet.

An unusual but most useful way of looking at a race is to imagine a moving staircase which is going down at a steady speed. A group are near the top of the staircase and it is a rule that they may climb up the steps no faster than the steps are moving down. The result is that they stay in the same place. Now, to make it difficult, they must close their eyes and carry on walking up the staircase at no more than the limit speed.

With eyes shut one may stumble and fall below the rest. On recovering he will be several steps below the others, yet he cannot climb back up to where they are because he is restricted to a maximum speed which only enables him to go the same speed up the staircase as it is going down – that is, if he now does as well as he can, which means no more slip-ups, he will only remain at the same point on the staircase. Each time he falters in his step or trips he will drop lower down the staircase. If he falls flat on his face he will end up at the bottom.

The one who remains nearest the top of the staircase is the one who falters least, makes fewest mistakes. The one who ends up nearest the bottom makes most mistakes, or certainly the most serious ones. The others in the group will be spread between these extremes according to the number and seriousness of their mistakes. Even the leader, unless he is perfect, will not remain at his starting point on the staircase. He too will make small errors, but they will be fewer than everyone else's.

This is exactly what happens in a sailing race, assuming everyone is in one-design boats which have no individual speed differences. The ideal race is one which is rarely, if ever, sailed and is the equivalent of our blind stair-walker remaining on the top step – a flawless performance.

Not even the Pattissons and Elvströms can truly reach perfection, though they often come as close as makes no difference. The fellow who falls flat on his face and has to be picked up off the floor at the bottom of the staircase . . . well, we've all capsized during a race, or been disqualified. For the most part results usually lie between these two extremes.

Viewing a race in this way shows that you rely for gaining places less on your own brilliance than on other people's errors. If you sail as closely as possible to the ideal race (staying very nearly on that top step) you win because of the imperfections in everyone else. In going for improvement in race results you should, therefore, be removing all possible imperfections, mistakes if you like, from your sailing technique rather than aiming primarily to beat everyone else. Whether you beat everyone else or not is only a measure of how successful you have been in perfecting your sailing abilities.

So far no account has been taken of boat tune. It has been assumed that boats are all totally one-design. Yet in all but the strictest one-designs there are marked differences in the inherent speed of individual class boats. These differences, though, do not invalidate this approach. Using the moving staircase analogy, we now have a group of people whose climbing speeds are all slightly different. One man still climbs at exactly the same speed as the staircase moves downwards, so stays on the top step (he represents the best tuned, fastest boat in the fleet). Another's climbing speed is noticeably slower, so that even without mistakes or imperfections he will end up several steps below his starting position (the slowest boat in the fleet). All the others fall between these extremes. Inherent boat speed, therefore, provides a narrow handicap scheme within class racing. The helmsman in the fastest boat has a few mistakes to spare over the slowest. That is all.

Boat speed differences are in reality more often differences in helmsman speed. But as we all have a bit of blamery in us we talk about having less boat speed than someone else, not less helmsman speed. In fact someone with excellent helming technique will make a boat sail through the water noticeably faster than someone of only moderate ability.

These differences in helmsman speed really showed up when the Laser epidemic hit us. Previously speed differences could more easily be put down to boat tune, but the Laser removed that variable. If one helmsman was going faster than another of similar weight, it was because he was sailing his boat faster. And you have only to see the great distances that open up between the leaders and tail-enders in Laser fleets to appreciate that helmsman speed is a major factor in deciding who wins races.

When the Laser first appeared, some sailors were convinced that there were appreciable differences in boat speed. One helmsman in my own club was certain a friend of his was beating him because he had a faster Laser. To prove his point he persuaded his friend to swap boats for one race. But in that race the boats' positions were reversed – his friend still beat him in the 'slow' boat. Within a few months this slower helmsman had switched to a class where the slow boat theory was an accepted visa to the land of mediocrity, for he was a confirmed 'blamer'.

Blaming other things than yourself for indifferent performance is a vital element in the coach/sailor idea. If you have your roles as coach and sailor separated out, the sailor's job is finished once the race is over and the coach then takes charge. While the sailing-self views mistakes and flaws as impediments to success, which during the race they are, the coach has a much longer term view and looks on the tactical errors and imperfections in technique not with hostility, but with a critical eye. To the coach these errors are lessons through which improvement will come: eliminate each error from the sailing-self and improved results will automatically follow. The helmsman who is not in the habit of looking at his racing in this way fails to make the best use of his own experience.

The helmsman who is a 'blamer' does make some use of his experience, but very unproductive use. His performing, sailing-self tries to improve his performance in everyone else's eyes after the race is over by describing to anyone prepared to listen (however reluctantly) a mass of misfortunes, which prevented the best man winning. So interested is he in compensating for the damage his ego suffered by not achieving the success it desired on the water, that he just doesn't get round to an objective analysis of his performance, but stays with his subjective, performing self, still striving to recoup some prestige from the lost race.

No-one is convinced. Except, to some extent at least, the blamer himself. And so he constructs a barrier to his own improvement. He has exorcised his mistakes from that race by talking them away. But that does not help in the long term. He has not eliminated them from his repertoire of sailing skills. Given the same circumstances next time he will make the same mistakes again and, as often as not, follow up afterwards with the same excuses. He has become too completely the performing-self, excluding the coach in him who would be able to look at the race objectively and work out ways of eliminating tomorrow the flaws which deprived the peforming-self of victory today.

Take for example a place lost by our blamer friend just short of the finish line in a close-tacking duel. A boat behind approaches the finish on starboard tack; our friend must put in a tack close under his lee bow to back-wind him and finish ahead. The tack turns out badly because the crew gets tangled up and fails to uncleat the jib, which remains aback just long enough to let the other boat break the lee bow and finish ahead.

No doubt about blame there – the crew. And our friend may feel much better after letting the crew (and anyone else within earshot) know who's fault it was. But does that prevent the same thing from happening in a tight spot during some future race? Not at all. Unless the bad tack was completely exceptional it is going to recur, most probably again at a tactically crucial moment.

A helmsman who looks more analytically at that bad tack will see that bad tacks do occur from time to time when the pressure is on. Perhaps this realization comes when driving home as he re-runs the key points of the race through his mind. Can the same thing be stopped from happening in future? Yes, he realizes, quite simply. He and his crew will go out half an hour early for the next three or four races and spend the extra time practising coming about until they can make perfect tacks with their eyes shut.

This is the approach which produces improvement, and it can be applied successfully to everything that happens while racing. The question 'Why did I lose?' is, when asked relentlessly and in a really probing way, the most powerful long-term race-winning weapon available to you. The reasons the coach discovers for your losing today are the lessons which, when thoroughly absorbed by the sailor, will enable you to win tomorrow.

3 A plan of attack

If you are seriously interested in improving your racing results and enjoyment, stop, think and start again. Your new approach should be more analytical, more positive, more thorough and more objective. Now I am going to make all this usefully practical and show how anyone can use these ideas on their own sailing to produce the maximum amount of improvement for a given amount of time and effort. The more time and effort you give, of course, the faster the improvement.

What you need to push your improvement along is a plan of attack – a system which will enable you to work step by manageable step through the problems that must be overcome in learning to win races. Reaching that goal, provided you have a plan, then becomes a question of time and the perseverance to go step-by-step along the route. The plan need not be too rigid, but it should be well thought out to define the most immediate problems and give ways of overcoming them.

Nor need you look for immediate short-term success (though that may come); it is long-term improvement that is the aim. If you can think in terms of a season's improvement rather than any instant success, you should have the right time scale for the plan I'm going to explain. Shorter-term plans of, say, three months are feasible, but a longish time scale is preferable since this is a campaign, a series of battles, rather than an isolated, one-off attack.

What are you aiming for?

To start with it is a good idea to decide on the goal. You need a realistic target which you can work towards with enthusiasm; one which is beyond you at the moment, but not impossibly so – a target which might reasonably be attained after six months' steady effort.

A good target for a helmsman and crew that finish around tenth on their good days in their class's open events and in the thirties on their poorer days would be to aim for a place in the top five on their good days and to remain in the top fifteen on their poorer days. This is not an unreasonable improvement to go for over six months. The target is not likely to be too ambitious and so cause disappointment – an important point, because disappointment can cause people to give up trying.

To take another example, a club fleet may be split between a small group at the front who share the winning and the rest who don't. A good target for a tail-endish helmsman in his second season of racing would be to beat the other non-winners regularly. This is a realistic standard which he can work towards with enthusiasm. If he worked well he might get close by the end of the season or even achieve success before that. Either way he'd have made good progress and could set himself a higher target the following season.

Notice that the target for the back or middle-of-the-fleet helmsman was not to win outright, but to win against other non-winners. If he had planned to start winning races by the end of the season he'd very likely have become disheartened before the season was over. So you should make a winnable race-within-a-race, not a mammoth task like trying to thrash the club champion within six months. Improvement is then a gradual business which, if not always spectacular, is certain.

There is a trap here which should be avoided Most people do set themselves private targets anyway; these take the form of helmsmen they usually race against who are about the same standard or marginally faster. These are poor targets to choose. In the first place the objective is not ambitious enough – you are looking for substantial, season-long improvement, not marginal gains. And in the second place, measuring your performance against particular individuals makes you over-aware of the competitive hierarchy and creates serious psychological barriers to improvement as I shall explain in Chapter 15.

Gauge yourself instead by your overall place in the fleet. That is much better than being limited to measuring yourself against any particular individual. The general standard two-thirds of the way down a club fleet is fairly constant. The standard of two or three individuals is not, and you get a false impression of your performance on the days when they are sailing badly. Think beyond the immediate, localized group of helmsmen you at present race against and you will go beyond it. Think only within that group and you will stay within it.

The same kind of target setting holds good for national and international competition. There too, the standard must always be challenging, but not over-ambitious. And most important, at whatever level, the target should be geared to the amount of time and effort you are prepared to put into improving your racing. If you set yourself an ambitious target then you must also set yourself an ambitious self-teaching programme to achieve it.

Even so, the target is nothing more than a yardstick, a means of measuring improvement. You don't *have* to reach it, though it's good if you do. It's a way of keeping up a high incentive for improvement without being completely demoralized by the seemingly unattainable speed of the champions. The target keeps you working at your immediate problems and, by putting those behind you, moving on to new ones as you improve until, if you have a real love of sailing, perseverance and aptitude, you can put even the champions behind you.

A self-set target is therefore a useful but not essential first stage in a sailing improvement programme, and no-one should get obsessed by it. The next stage, though, is essential. The average sailor tends to ignore the next step, but it is something over which anyone who has taken home major sailing trophies has taken a good deal of time and trouble.

Getting your priorities right

If the fastest way to improve is to throw imperfections overboard the detailed sailing tasks must be raised to a higher level of perfection. And to do that you must first identify which of the many skills and abilities of racing you most need to work on – in other words, what your priorities are.

It is important at this point to take on the role of being your own coach as completely as possible. Don't assume you know what needs to be put right with your sailing, but look at your techniques as though they were someone else's. Keep a really open mind during this assessment of your sailing abilities and you might get some surprises.

For those who are in only their first or second season's racing, pinpointing weakness is not as vital. Instead, several different methods can be combined with regular racing: solo practice, perhaps a week-long racing course, some reading, paired practice, observation and perhaps some crewing. Doing more of these other activities and less racing provides a general, all-round boost to performance. After a time specific weaknesses will emerge and these can be dealt with by self-coaching.

One of the biggest difficulties facing potentially successful helmsmen is to recognize their own weaknesses. They may think they know the ways in which they could most usefully improve, but they are usually wrong – which is why effort given to improving results may have little or no effect on performance, however hard a helmsman tries. It is crucial to identify the key problems, so it is well worth taking time off to do a thorough analysis, step-by-step.

A good starting point is to ask yourself 'What don't I like?' – heavy weather, light air, shifting winds, navigation, the crew, big fleets, starts, sailing through waves and so on. The possibilities are legion. To help you in this assessment, here's a checklist of some of the commoner dislikes:

Heavy weather generally	Light air generally
Heavy weather running	Gybing
Heavy weather reaches	Capsizing
Shifting winds	Heavy weather beating
Sailing through waves	Close fetching legs
Practising outside races	Rock steady winds (ie boat speed contests)
Covering duels	Short tacking against a current
Rules freaks	Aggressive opponents
Working on your boat	

- Light air starts
- Heavy weather starts
- Downwind starts
- Mass starts
- Big fleets
- International competition
- One or more arch-rivals who always manage to out-do you
- Holding on to a lead
- Doing well when it really matters
- Racing in very changeable conditions
- Having an incident or mistake happen which badly affects the rest of your race
- Close tactics with other boats
- Boat tuning
- Starts generally
- Mark roundings
- Tidal starts
- Biased starting lines
- Racing away from home
- Gate starts
- Reading sailing instructions and courses
- Windward tactics
- Long races
- The rules
- Spinnaker work
- Navigation
- Night sailing
- The crew
- Protests
- Pre-race planning

That's quite a list to be going on with but it's by no means complete and you may be able to add to it. Once you have gone through the list to see which items you don't like, try going through it again picking out those which cause you to do badly or lose you places. The two often go together.

The reason for that is that you tend to like and enjoy what you are best at, and as you give more thought and practice to these things you are most likely to improve them. By working instead at what you like least and are worst at, you get a more balanced approach. When working on the things you are worst at, you tend to improve more rapidly, since it is far easier to take something done indifferently and learn to do it well than take something you do well and learn to do it very well. The nearer to perfection you get, the more the law of diminishing returns sets in.

There is one great bonus in singling out weaknesses for treatment – more enjoyment. As the things you are weakest at improve, you start to enjoy them. Tacking, if done indifferently, is a tedious chore which must be gone through every time you want to change boards on a beat. Fluent, flawless tacking, on the other hand, is a real pleasure, a delight, as you flow through a rhythmic sequence which takes you effortlessly from one tack to the other. Average tacking and flawless tacking are worlds apart: one is a chore and gains you nothing, the other a harmony of balance and movement, an art form, which will also win you races.

Basic tactics are affected, too. Flawless tacking provides the freedom to switch tacks without a second's thought when the tactical situation demands; average tacking means that a tack will always be put off until it can't conveniently be delayed any longer. So by bringing tacking skills up to a high level, a chain reaction sets in which ensures that other sailing abilities are automatically helped. No one skill exists in isolation and our sailing skills interlock in such a way that by working up one skill we improve another, whether we are aware of it or not. Which is most fortunate, since we now have to narrow down our problem list to a very small number of items.

Three problem areas are quite enough to deal with at once, so pick three separate areas to work on. No more than that. According to one of the most authoritative and comprehensive books ever written on sport, the East German *Track and Field* (Kimpton, 1956): 'one thing a coach should never do is draw attention to several mistakes simultaneously.' So pick areas which are quite separate. One might be wave technique, another starting, another mark-rounding.

For the moment, remember, do no more than select the problem areas, taking time to do so without worrying about how to work on them, since that might influence your choice. Take time off from racing to do this – perhaps a couple of weeks. Get out in a rescue boat during a race or two and study what everyone is doing, especially what the people who usually beat you are doing. Watch how they helm their boats, how they tack, how they have their sails set, how they start, how and where they sit, how they work their boats upwind, downwind. Everything. Study just as closely how someone of exactly your own standard is doing these same things and compare his performance with the champion's. In detail.

For several seasons I spent many weeks watching racing at all levels from the spectacularly incompetent to the perfection of the Olympics and learnt a tremendous amount just from looking. Provided you're in reasonable racing trim yourself and you really keep your eyes open, it is surprising what you can pick up. There is no boat to handle; there are no tactics to worry about. Instead you can look hard to see exactly what the front-runners are doing that puts them up there, and what the less good are doing that stops them being at the front.

All this is part of assessing what most needs to be worked on in your racing. If you think you know already without all that, or reckon I'm making too much of the whole priorities business, take a look at one area many helmsmen will have included in their top three problem areas: boat tune.

The boat tune trap

Boat tune seems a good, safe item because it's never perfect and it holds out the same promise as football pools – getting something no-one else has for next to nothing, an unfair advantage. Besides, it's tangible. You can move things around and tinker away to your heart's content. But if boat tune is on your list, beware . . .

Before I went to university I raced quite successfully at my local club, winning occasional races and some open events, but never managing to win consistently in all weathers. Modesty was not an attribute I possessed in measurable quantity so I believed my proper position to be first in every race. I worked hard to achieve that, but still that breakthrough into consistent winning didn't happen.

Then I went to London University, where one or two of the finest helmsmen in the country were racing Fireflies. At my home club of Bassenthwaite in the North of England I had been sailing GP14s, which in the best racing circles were spoken about either not at all or impolitely. So I was coming from the wrong class in the wrong part of the country and not winning regularly either. I was obviously going to have to crew for a year to learn to sail as well as the University first team who then, as now, were almost as good as they told everyone they were.

To my own and everyone else's astonishment I managed second place in the first of the University championship points races. Naturally I'd been lucky. Next race I was even luckier and won. In fact I kept on being lucky and by the end of the winter I'd won the points series. And luck, by then, had been recognized as something else – good old-fashioned sailing ability. It turned out that I was better at sailing than I'd thought I was. Four years later I discovered why.

After university I returned to my home club, equipped myself with a new GP14 and started the season's racing. I won the first race, the second, third . . . right through the season. Suddenly that winning streak I'd been seeking four years earlier had come. Certainly

I'd learned a thing or two at university but the most important change was the boat. The earlier one had been slow; not deperately slow, but slow enough to provide a constant handicap.

In the short term the slowness of the boat had prevented my results being better, but in the long term I became a better sailor. I had assumed I was losing because I wasn't a good enough sailor to win, so I worked on those sailing abilities which were letting me down until they didn't let me down any more. The result was that when I got myself a boat which was at least as fast as the best in the fleet it really took off.

Had I assumed that the boat was preventing me from doing better in those pre-university days, I might well have achieved some better results by improving the efficiency of rig and hull. The work would then have been put into the boat rather than my basic sailing ability. When I went to university I would have left the boat and all that work behind. As it was I left the boat behind and brought the work with me in the shape of helming skills. It was possible to step into different classes and go fast. The skills of fine tuning could be learned later.

And the one essential for fine boat tuning is fine helming. All the finest racing helmsmen grew up in one-design classes where differences in boat speed are marginal and where helmsmanship matters above all else. There may be some helmsmen who didn't get to the top that way, but I don't know of any.

Ideally, we should bring everything to a high degree of excellence at the same rate, and I certainly made the mistake of letting sail and boat tune fall behind everything else. Better that, though, than to have spent valuable time and effort working on the boat when the essential sailing skills just weren't sufficiently developed to have enabled me to do well, even in the unlikely event of my ending up with the fastest boat in the fleet.

Often there is an element of blamery in deciding to spend time and effort working up boat tune. Mostly the problem is of helmsman and crew tune. Only if you're pretty sure the boat is wrong should you have boat tune on your list. Otherwise leave it off, and if it really is a problem it will find its way onto a future list. If you are going to tackle boat tune you should really be prepared to get stuck into learning about sail shapes, spreader effects, mast bend, fairlead positions, centreboard slots and the whole detailed business of making the machine as efficient as it can be in any particular strength of wind.

For anyone in the middle or tail end of a club fleet, working on boat tune is usually unnecessary. Basic sail setting-up and trimming matter far more. If boat tune is a problem at this level, solve it with a tape measure. Set everything to be the same as the club champion and go from there.

Fine boat tune doesn't count for much in shifting winds or in extreme conditions – either very heavy weather or very light air. It matters most in steady winds and among helmsmen of very similar ability. Then it can be crucial, and the higher your standard the more fine boat tune matters. Until then it pays to keep the boat and its layout as simple as possible and get on with learning how to acquire the skills and racing knowledge which give . . . boat speed? No, helmsman speed.

4 The art of learning

When you have taken the advice given in the last chapter and, after much heart-searching, established to your own dissatisfaction that your tacking/starting/wave technique/heavy weather skill/thinking/racing in general could be greatly improved you can do one of the following:

Nothing
Hope it will get better on its own
Decide to improve whatever isn't so good – but later
Decide to improve whatever isn't so good – now
Take up golf

The rest of this book is for the benefit of those who opt for either of the last two choices, since anyone taking those choices is concerned enough about his sailing to do something positive – even giving it up. When you go deeply into the best ways of learning to succeed in competition you find the same basic truths, whether the sport is sailing, high diving or golf, there are ways you can work on a skill or ability so that it can't help but improve.

Look at the way most helmsmen learn their racing. They buy a boat, learn to sail, become interested in racing and join the back of the fleet. Improvement comes mainly through racing and probably some reading about how the experts race their boats. Little or no effort is made to work on individual skills and repeated racing is seen to be the way to improve. Some start as crews for the more expert, which accelerates their learning so that they go quickly up to mid-fleet or even higher. However a helmsman begins, at some point his progress levels off and he reaches the peak to which his natural abilities and his normal, but thoroughly inefficient, learning of the sport have limited him.

His natural abilities are a limitation which he can do nothing about; but anyone would be wrong to assume that it is his natural abilities which are restraining him from doing better. Virtually no-one has reached the point where he is using his natural abilities to the full, and most of those who come close to doing so have names that are familiar to those who read the yachting press. Anyone who falls into the trap of saying to himself, 'I just don't have the natural ability to win my races' thereby ensures that he won't win them. Unless he's sailing at the top international level he is almost certainly wrong: anyone who enjoys the sport and is not suffering from some physical or mental disability has what it takes to win club races and do well nationally. Claiming inability is just a subtle form of 'blamery'.

All of us have far greater capabilities within us than we recognize; what we must do is coach ourselves in such a way that those capabilities can come out. Instead of the usual way of learning to race more successfully we can use a far more effective, perfectionist approach.

The basic problem with most people's racing is that the detailed work of perfecting skills is never tackled from the start. Since learning is usually done by repeatedly racing, techniques which were wrongly learned early on tend not to reach perfection but stick about 70 per cent of the way there, or maybe 80 per cent or 85 per cent. And if someone is not racing successfully it is because the detailed tasks required to sail the boat efficiently round the course are being done imperfectly.

An expert coach who could help break the deadlock would be a solution, but there aren't many of those about. The alternative is to take the self-coaching job seriously and understand the whole business of learning. Besides, by learning to become a coach you can do the job very successfully yourself.

To see how complex mental and physical skills can most efficiently be learned and perfected I'm going to turn to another field altogether – concert piano playing. Playing the piano to concert standard has much in common with top level sailing, though the pianist's task is even harder. Concert pianists have to develop a phenomenally high degree of muscular co-ordination and control to do apparently impossible physical feats with the highest degree of artistry. The whole mind, body and spirit are involved and the powers of concentration required, to succeed, are total. Pianists also have to bring out their best when the pressures are greatest, perhaps before a concert hall audience of 2,000 and five million television viewers.

The pianist's artistry might be largely inborn, but the physical skills and necessary mental control to perform flawlessly under enormous psychological pressure are learned. The methods used in teaching concert pianists have been developed over the years and are far ahead of those so far used for training even Olympic sailors. The vast majority of sailors use poor learning methods similar to those of the average amateur pianist. You can therefore learn a lot by studying how concert pianists train, recognizing how their basic learning methods differ from those commonly used.

Fifteen years ago I had the perfect opportunity to see a top flight pianist's working methods; I became very close friends with someone who happened to be one. She had been a child prodigy, playing the solo part in a concerto before an audience of 2,000 when she was only ten years old. Being a moderate amateur pianist myself, I estimated the number of hours I had spent on the piano stool and compared that to the time my friend had spent acquiring the ability to play professional concerts by the age of ten.

Surprisingly, my friend had spent fewer hours getting to concert standard than I had spent struggling to reach my mediocre amateur level. So either she was born vastly more talented at piano playing, or the way I had learned was far less efficient than the way she had learned. Certainly she had more natural talent, but not that much more. The big difference lay in the learning methods – and especially in the way she practised.

The most noticeable difference was that, whereas I struggled at my practising, she didn't. I went all out at a new piece, rushing into it with lots of enthusiasm and wrong notes, trying to get it to sound like the finished piece as fast as possible. She did exactly the opposite.

Instead of taking the piece as a whole, she broke it down into its smallest parts and worked on these, practising often with separate hands, slowly and in deliberately varied rhythms to familiarize her hands thoroughly with the notes. Individual difficulties would be singled out for special treatment. A difficult leap would be made more difficult by practising it with the eyes closed.

She worked efficiently, but as though time were unimportant. She never rushed herself yet in the long run things were learned more quickly as a result. The emphasis was always on perfection. Practising note perfect came before trying to play passages quickly. Perfection of the tiniest details was what counted until perfection itself became a habit.

The work went on five hours a day, six and even seven days a week. When a passage went wrong during practice, she didn't mentally beat herself with a stick and get angry but merely went over it again, maybe more slowly, or homed in on the particular difficulty that had tripped her up and worked on that. If something was especially difficult she would find a variety of ways of working at the difficulty until, after several weeks, it was no longer a difficulty. And when the time came to perform a piece, it never had to be memorized: the muscles already knew it, note perfect. The intricate details of the performance were simply put onto automatic pilot, leaving her mind and emotions free to control, shape and breathe life into the music, and, when inspiration truly flowed, surrender herself to the perfection that was there.

Compare that with the way most people learn to race sailing boats. Like the amateur pianist, they don't worry much about the detail but get as quickly as possible to the point where they can sail a whole race reasonably and then, mainly by repeatedly racing, gradually improve. In spite of a keen desire to reach greater heights, progress is thwarted by poor learning methods which make improvement slow and frustrating.

The result is that the helmsman and crew get along quite nicely until perhaps their second or third season. They are neither brilliant nor are they disgracing themselves. But like the amateur pianist, they are not improving noticeably either and begin to get used to the idea, whether they like it or not, that this is about as good as they'll ever be. The levelling off may happen later and higher, possibly after ten years from starting when not quite good enough to win a national championship, but at some point the competitor will reach a certain standard and stick at that particular level.

Applying more patient and perfectionist learning methods isn't particularly difficult. The main difficulty is breaking learning habits which have been acquired at school and elsewhere and replacing those by better ones. This is where you have really got to put your coaching hat on and start taking an interest in the exact methods you could use to race better, and how to apply these methods on yourself. Learning any skill is an art in itself. Some people have it naturally, others do not. Fortunately, the art can be acquired. Here are some ways in which it can be done:

Perfection in the smallest detail From perfection of the detail comes perfection of the whole. When everything in your sailing repertoire is done perfectly you stay on the top step of the moving stairway.

Patient, steady, long term progress is the aim Achieving perfection in the smaller details takes time. The whole process of learning takes time. If you try to rush it you get slapdash, end up learning more slowly and only ever get the skill 90 per cent perfect.

Learning a physical skill happens mainly when you are resting Learning is largely a subconscious process, especially when the skill is complex and involves the whole mind and body. Practising a skill is primarily a process of showing the subconscious what is involved and allowing it to acquire the ability to master the skill. Trying too hard at a difficult skill for a long time is the wrong way to work. The right way is to do short practice sessions regularly over several weeks or months.

Muscles have memories Muscular memory takes time to develop, so the learning process must allow time for this, which is again why a slower perfectionist approach to learning produces better long term results. Once a skill has been properly learned it is there to be drawn on without any conscious effort or struggle. A well-learned tack is automatically a perfect tack, you don't have to concentrate on *making* it a perfect tack; it already is. During a race the mind should not *strive* for the perfect tack but, when the learning has been properly done, let go into the perfect tack; the mind is then free to concentrate on other matters, such as other boats, tidal considerations or sail trim.

Isolate one skill at one time and work on that Single-mindedness in practice automatically produces single-minded racing. And if you are single-minded enough you can achieve anything. To perfect one part of the whole you must isolate that part and work towards perfection of that on its own. In that way you can centre yourself for short periods on that one ability and bring it to a high level of excellence. That process repeated on each skill in turn is how you can learn best.

The more ways we can find to work on a particular skill the better Different ways of working at one skill make the learning faster, easier and more complete. More of the whole person is brought to bear on the difficulty and success often just seems to come. It's as though the subsconscious learns best when it is shown the problem from all angles.

In practice a difficulty should be made even more difficult A force five is child's play when you have been sailing often in force six. Pianists introduce tricky rhythms into their practice which make technical difficulties more difficult. Then, during the pressures of performance the difficulty has gone. Fine boat control becomes second nature once you have learned to sail well on all points without a rudder.

When working to improve a skill it may get worse before it gets better Old habits must fall away before new ones can take their place. Part of the learning process is to experiment with different ways of doing the job. If it isn't right at the moment it must be re-learned; and you must go back to the start. You will be worse at the task to begin with, but more nearly perfect in the end.

Don't judge severely while learning This is the most difficult learning habit of them all to break. If you mentally chastise yourself every time you slip up during practice, you are inhibiting the learning which is going on subsconsciously. You are not so much practising to *make* the skill come right, as practising to enable the subconscious *to acquire* the skill. Impatient practice is bad.

Balanced learning Obsession with one facet, boat tune for example, means that the learning is unbalanced and other abilities are left to stagnate and deteriorate. When the learning is balanced, improvement in one area helps others, so progress is faster and easier.

Learning should be enjoyable Enjoyment is the most important thing in sailing, so it would be totally wrong to suggest learning methods which were not enjoyable. A mix of learning methods which you enjoy doing is essential. Then learning is faster, and so rewarding.

Learning a sailing skill

To show how these more perfectionist ways of learning can be applied in sailing, I shall take one basic dinghy racing skill and see how someone new to dinghy racing would ideally work to acquire that skill. It doesn't matter whether you race a sailboard, a Class 1 ocean racer or whether the class you race requires this skill; it is not the skill itself that is important, but the way of acquiring it. The skill which is going to be worked on is sailing a dinghy exactly upright in heavy weather – something very few can do, though many may think they can.

The first thing the learner should do is look: see what sailing upright is and how it's done. That can save months of trial and error. The idea is to watch heavy weather racing at close quarters from a rescue boat, looking to see how people keep their boats level, noticing all the detailed movements, recognizing what the heelers do that makes their boats heel.

An enormous amount can be learned in this way, especially on a gusty day, since gusts make it more difficult to hold the boat flat. He would see that the leaders hold their boats very level, even in the gusts. The middle of the fleet heel a little in the steady wind and more in the gusts. The back markers heel more all the time and get flattened in the gusts. He would see just how much ground boats that heel lose, and begin to realize how important upright sailing is for making a dinghy travel fast in a blow.

Our man might then be inclined to go off racing as usual and give special attention to sailing as upright as possible. That would be the normal way, but there is a better one. If you are going to improve one skill you should try to isolate it and tackle it on its own. There is enough to think about during a race as it is: tactics, the luff of the jib, physical exhaustion, people trying to do nasty things like overtake, no end of problems. So if our man has a score to settle with heeling he'd better get heeling on its own and settle the argument privately. That way he's sure of winning.

During the race he watched, people were generally having trouble because they were heeling to leeward, so the best way for our man to start his practising is to do the opposite – deliberately sail heeled to windward. He should get his boat sailing to windward as usual with him and his crew sitting out hard and then, by feathering up a little into the wind and maybe easing the mainsheet slightly, heel the boat 10° to windward and hold her there. It is important now to stay sitting out hard and sail to windward as though racing, but with that 10° of windward heel.

At coaching sessions I often have a whole group doing this deliberate heeling practice and most of them have big surprises. Several will say that their boats no longer have weather helm. Others look far better sailors than they did earlier in the day, as they sail their practice beats beautifully upright – though they believe they are heeling to windward.

When doing the windward heeling exercise our learner should get used to holding his boat at a steady 10° of windward heel all the time, sitting out hard and varying only the mainsheet and tiller to balance the forces in the rig. In lighter winds he can practise single-handed or with the crew sitting to leeward, again with the same angle of windward heel. He can also practise the windward heel when reaching and running (which can be most stimulating in force six).

The practice shouldn't go on for long – around half an hour or forty minutes at the most – and it should be broken up with brief rest periods of a minute or two, when the helmsman and crew simply let the sheets right out, allow the boat to lie beam on to the wind and take a breather before carrying on. These rest periods are part of the learning.

Time is on your side whenever you are working on a sailing skill so there is no need to rush. What you are doing is acquiring new habits and these take time to establish, just as old ones take time to fall away. One practice session for perfecting the 10° windward heel is therefore nothing like enough. Our man's best plan will be to carry on with his normal racing, but to put in two half hour spells of windward heeling practice each week for several weeks until it becomes second nature. Then he can practise sailing dead upright.

When doing this very basic practice it is important to pay attention to what everything feels like – to be aware of the pull of the tiller, the tensions in the legs and body due to sitting out, the wind on the face and head, the feeling of thighs on the side of the boat and the sounds the boat and the rig make. If you sail with more than just eyes and arms, and become more aware of the other senses while sailing they help in many more ways than you realize. As Elvström has said, 'If you only sailed with your eyes, anyone could do it.' A more complete bodily and mental awareness enables you to be one with the boat and thus become a more natural sailor. Regular and careful practice of the exercise over two or three months will also increase powers of concentration.

Doing windward heeling and upright sailing practice regularly will help heavy weather racing in other, unexpected ways. Even many experienced racing helmsmen have problems controlling the boat when a gust first strikes: they lose power and speed. But when you heel to windward just before the arrival of a sharp gust you accelerate and the boat is far more easily controlled. Our learner doesn't need to be told that. He will find out for himself during his practice stints and will automatically start using the technique during races. Within a month or two he could therefore be using a ploy that many who have raced for years have not learned.

Handling the beginning of gusts is something the learner could learn about by reading the right books, but even though he has been told how to do it, he doesn't know until he actually gets out onto the water and puts that theory into practice. He might know with his mind, but to do it he has also to know with his body and senses. By doing the windward heeling practice he learns more about the handling of gusts than he could expect to put into practice from books. By doing the practice and reading the right books he would learn just about everything there is to know about handling gusts. Quite quickly too.

To hold the windward heel rock steady it is necessary to keep glancing upwind to check whether any gusts are coming. As our man persevered with the exercise he wouldn't need to be told this. Provided he was really trying to perfect the skill, he would discover that gusts upset his balance but that they can also be seen on the water. During a race there is so much going on that, even if he had read in a book that he should look upwind to read the water for gusts, he'd have too much on his mind to bother. Even if he did bother he would probably have a serious problem in sailing his fastest windward course as soon as his eyes were off the jib.

Regular practice is therefore the way to test ideas picked up from reading. Once you have tried out some of the techniques you have read about, you can incorporate the better ones into your own racing repertoire. This can speed up progress appreciably.

In a later chapter on heavy weather racing, for example, I say that once a gust has passed you should not bear away into the lull but should pinch up into the beginning of the lull. That is my advice; other authors have said the opposite. Who is right? The way to find out is for our learner (by now a very fast learner) to try both methods and then decide for himself. Then he uses the advice given in the book to extend his own racing knowledge and technique by personal experience. And whether he proves me right or wrong doesn't matter. The advice enables him to refine his racing skill – whether that advice was right for him and his class of boat or not.

By singling out one ability, in this case the ability to keep a boat dead level in a strong wind and devoting some long-term, regular effort towards perfecting that one skill you can develop it to a high degree of perfection fairly quickly. Other abilities automatically improve at the same time.

More importantly, though, you develop the habit of practising for perfection if that is kept up, perfection itself becomes a habit. And that is what really produces success. Paul Elvström continually emphasizes the importance of being a perfectionist in sailing. 'If you are a perfectionist,' he says, 'you want to do things very correctly, very precisely, very accurately. I think that is the way to be fast.' He may be wrong, but if he is, he has done unusually well by being wrong.

5 Ways of learning

If your racing is not improving or improving only slowly it is, as I said right at the beginning, not because you are failing yourself as a sailor but because you are failing as a sailing coach.

Racing and learning to race are two fundamentally different things. Some racing is necessary for improvement, but an excess of it can be a serious barrier. We therefore need to take a close look at the other learning methods which can be used to perfect your racing ability. There are twelve ways altogether, of which racing itself is only one. In the last chapter only three ways were used to work on upright sailing: observation, reading and solo practising. There are nine others; we were dealing with only one of the countless skills that constitute racing. The possibilities that open up are enormous.

It is often said that the best way to learn something is to teach it, and that is what you are going to be doing – but with yourself. This chapter is for your coaching-self, who will then apply the most effective and well thought-out coaching methods to the sailor-self, methods which will produce the most improvement for the least effort. Here, then, are the basic coaching tools that are available, the twelve learning methods.

Race experience

Many people rely on racing as virtually their only way of learning to race more successfully. Yet race experience alone is of limited value. More racing does not necessarily mean better results. Often it brings the opposite. Many people find that on coming back after a break they do better to begin with, perhaps just in the first race or even the first part of that race. Race experience alone when not backed up by other ways of learning can actually hold a helmsman back from further improvement, and very often does – without the helmsman realizing what is happening. It works like this.

To improve a technique, tacking for example, you must experiment. Experimenting means that you will be doing some worse tacks than usual. These bad tacks are inevitable; you won't learn to do flawless tacks without first doing many disastrous ones. Yet, you already have a tacking method which gets you by. It isn't the best there is, but it's reliable and you are fairly comfortable with it. During a race you are reluctant to experiment because, if you are trying to do well, it would be crazy deliberately to do something which you know would make you do worse. Wouldn't it? So you go through the mediocre tack every time you go about. And every time you do the mediocre tack you become more comfortable with it, until eventually it feels right. But it isn't right. Not if you want to improve the quality of your racing.

So normal race experience on its own tends to confirm you in what you are doing already. Provided you are going out to win, that is. But aren't you always entering races with the idea of winning if possible? Not if you are looking for long-term improvement. Some races can be used for learning. Simply accept that you are going to do worse than usual; what you are going to do instead is to use these races specifically to work on weaker areas. If tacking is one of these, then pay more attention to the quality of tacks than to your position at the end of the beat.

This may sound outrageous, but it is the way many champions work. You can't win every race you enter, so it's no bad thing to decide not to even try to win some of the less important ones but to use them instead as a classroom. The lessons learned may then be applied to the races you do want to win.

Rodney Pattisson is the master of this strategy. In the 1975 British Open Flying Dutchman championship Pattisson finished third in almost every race, being soundly beaten by the Pajot brothers of France and Wolf of East Germany. Often Pattisson was over three minutes behind the winner. With just over a year left to the Olympics I was sceptical that he could bring his performance up sufficiently to be anywhere near gold medal-winning standard. I said as much to him and he replied with complete certainty that this was not an event which he'd gone into with much likelihood of winning, but we should wait till next year. We did. At Hyeres early in the summer he was well down the fleet, often in the twenties. At the Olympics four months later he won the silver medal. Afterwards I asked about Hyeres, and he said it had taught him a lot about his new boat and sails. Again, this was not an event that he had prepared himself to win. It was one which he was using for learning and practice. Other leading helmsmen use the same strategy, among them John Loveday, three times 505 world champion.

Using some races as classrooms gives greater freedom to experiment and learn. You can also avoid continually reinforcing old and bad habits, so keeping your sailing fresh, spontaneous and alive. It's then also fun. For example, a helmsman who always starts badly might want to know what a fantastic start feels like. In a race which he is treating purely as practice he might deliberately cross the line five seconds early. And he can still sail the race holding all rights under the rules. If he's not used to starting well, his first beat after the flying start may seem spectacularly good to him in clear wind for a change and, with nothing to lose, he may actually sail better than usual. Whatever happens he's likely to learn something he didn't know before. The one thing he won't get, though, is a finishing gun, but in a learning race that doesn't matter.

Deliberately starting 30 seconds late is an interesting experience for a helmsman who normally finishes high up, but who goes to pieces when he messes up his start. A deliberate late start will enable him to see how easy it can be to power through a fleet from behind. This self-imposed handicap automatically gives him a much more positive attitude to climbing up the fleet; any future messed up start will then be easier to get over and will not ruin his race.

A wide range of racing conditions is important for learning, especially racing away from home or at international events. Variety of sailing water and conditions matters more the nearer a helmsman is to the top of his class.

So race experience is an essential method of learning, but most can be gained from it if it is intelligently used and not over-indulged. Maximum benefit comes from a broad range of learning methods of which racing itself is only one.

Observation

If you can see – really see – what people who always beat you do, you are part of the way towards doing the same yourself. Those who have started along the lines already suggested and have watched a race or two will very likely have experienced some of the benefits of observing. If you put your mind to it, you can learn an enormous amount from the side lines.

Any question on your mind about your own sailing will often be answered by making a point of looking at how others handle the same problem. But looking means more than just taking on the job of race officer for the day; it is single-minded attention, comparing. Why has that boat just lost a place? How far from the centreline is the leader sheeting his boom on the beat? Does he play the mainsheet? When? How? Which way does his crew face when tacking: forwards or backwards? What about the jib setting and the slot between jib and mainsail – how does the champion have these? How does that compare with how someone of your own standard has them? How much tiller movement are people using upwind, downwind? And so on. The watching will produce the best results if beforehand you jot down a list of techniques or boat handling skills in your three chosen priority areas which you would most like to study.

Photographs can be useful too, though care is needed in analysing them. Rigs flex a good deal when sailing through waves, so if the bow is burying into a wave the mast will be much more bent than usual. A careful analysis of a magazine photograph of the national champion sailing his boat can sometimes tell you things which could help your own racing. Photographs of you racing your own boat can also be valuable; they may well show you something about your racing that you didn't know before. The Laser photographs in *Start To Win* (Adlard Coles, 1974) were specially taken of a friend and me staging a series of set pieces for the photographer. When my friend looked at the pictures he was astonished to see that at no time was he sailing his boat dead level. There was always about 10° of heel, yet he believed that he had been sailing plumb upright. It needed a photograph to tell him otherwise.

Video can also be a valuable tool for watching; especially when used on your own boat, since it's often possible to see wrong habits, and poorly co-ordinated movement or techniques which you hadn't previously been able to see yourself doing. Video can be used later on when the problem has been worked at to check whether it has been properly resolved. This technique can be used effectively to work on tacking, gybing and sail-changing on offshore yachts where good teamwork between crew members is crucial. Allowing a crew member to see himself getting it wrong is worth a month of bawling him out.

Solo practice

Practice outside races is the fastest and easiest way of improving a whole range of sailing skills and techniques. It also seems to open up in a helmsman those all-important intuitive qualities that every champion possesses.

In other sports many more hours are spent in practice than in competing, yet in sailing, private practice is relatively rare among adults. Among children, though, it's an epidemic, which goes a long way towards explaining how some of them quickly reach a high competitive standard. A few adults who are regarded as especially keen may often be seen out sailing alone or matching themselves against one other boat, but most adults believe that lots of racing is pretty well all that's required. Some don't, though, and it is hardly possible that Elvström, Melges and Bertrand are all wrong and that hours and hours practising before major events are unnecessary.

Solo practice is especially good for working on skills which are more intuitive and rely on 'feel', such as boat handling and heavy weather techniques; it automatically draws you into closer touch with the elements and your boat than is ever possible during the in-fighting and tensions of a race. The most important of these is a togetherness with the boat, the feeling of being totally at home in her, the feeling that rudder and mainsail are extensions of your arms and the hull part of your body.

The more you become one with the boat, the faster you go. It just happens. Certainly greater sensitivity to the wind and waves develops and all the senses involved in sailing become more the more time that is spent alone in the boat. Seeing, feeling, balance and hearing all become more totally attuned to the sailing and concentration automatically improves. When you are one with the boat your thoughts might stray from the task of sailing her as fast as possible, but concentration does not. The essential automatic pilot skill, that ability to keep the boat at peak performance while looking at other boats or the water upwind, develops through practising.

Practice is especially helpful when combined with reading. The practical and theoretical advice of experts means far more when you're able to try out what they say in a practice session; or, working the other way round, when some problem emerges while sailing you can look up how any of the experts deal with that same problem. That can short-cut hours of trial and error.

Practising is so important a part of learning to win that Chapter 11 is given over entirely to the subject.

Crewing

Crewing for a first class helmsman for a season is an excellent way of learning to become a first class helmsman yourself. By crewing you automatically acquire many of the helmsman's skills. When the helmsman is a good one you start off by learning good habits. This saves a lot of effort and time, since it cuts out a process that many established middle-of-the-fleet sailors have to go through – they must let go of bad habits they have acquired and supplant them with good habits.

The best way to use crewing as a learning method is to combine it with a fair amount of helming practice, but not necessarily in races. When in my teens I crewed often for my father, who was then a very fine dinghy helmsman, and he would often discuss the race afterwards, which meant I was able to learn by his mistakes, and so would often know the right thing to do later on when I began helming in races.

Crewing isn't vital, but if it can be worked into the scheme, so much the better. More is learned by a middle or back-of-the-fleet sailor crewing for the club champion in a race than by helming in that same race himself – provided of course he can crew competently, otherwise his learning could be confined to corrective vocabulary.

Physical fitness

Physical training should always be according to need. The need in sailing is only heavily physical in heavy weather. In light and medium air, sailing is not primarily a physical sport; all it needs is good average fitness; tough fitness training is no use for improving medium and light weather performance.

Physical fitness does contribute to alertness of mind and a general sense of well-being, but that can be had through regular fairly light exercising. It is certainly not true that the more the body is exercised the sharper the mind becomes. This subject is dealt with more thoroughly in Chapter 13 since there are many different ways in which you can train physically; some of the alternatives to the traditional gymnasium routines may be found more suitable for many sailors.

For many keen sailors, then, no special physical training is necessary. Regular sailing itself provides enough basic fitness for the needs of all but the more ambitious. Keeping fit in the winter when not sailing, though, is important to keep the body toned up. Most helmsmen sail to keep fit, not keep fit to sail. And that, for the majority, is the way to keep it.

Swapping boats and classes

There is a good deal to be learned from swapping boats with someone else for a weekend's club racing. The strange boat forces you to experiment with sail setting and sail trim, and at the same time someone is experimenting with your boat and rig. Comparison of notes after the weekend's sailing can bring up some interesting points about sail trim and the way the boat handles.

Switching to different classes is also a good way of learning, as Garry Hoyt, who has been at the front of several classes, explains in his book *Go for the Gold* (Nautical Publishing Company, 1972): 'The benefits of switching classes are more than just technical. It happens to be great fun to learn the quirks and idiosyncrasies of different boats. You will also find that each class emphasizes some particular skill, and if you learn that class you will have learned that particular skill better than anyone who has not sailed that class . . . Put your pride on the line in a new class. Your ego may take a few whacks, but you will find yourself forced to innovate where in your own class you might rely on habit – and a far stronger sailor emerges.'

It used to be thought that the best way to learn to helm any of the Ton class ocean racers was to sail Ton class ocean racers. Experience over the past few years has shown that the very best dinghy helmsmen have a disconcerting knack of being able to step into these boats and sail them remarkably fast in a very short time. Windsurfing is good practice for dinghy sailors; racing Lasers is good practice for windsurfer races. The wider the range of classes raced, the more cross-fertilization of the experiences in each, and the greater the benefit.

Paired practice

Matching yourself against one other boat of similar standard is excellent practice. Working together it is possible to improve boat speed, or helmsman speed, depending on which is deficient. Boat tune and adjustment can be refined by sailing long tacks together and making minor adjustments. Tacking skills can be worked on, in fact any part of a race can be practised, by sailing with just one other boat.

It is important to pool knowledge when working with another helmsman. In this way you both learn even faster. He can see things about your boat and sailing which could be improved; he finds things about his own sailing which he has picked up during the practice session and he tells you. You tell him everything you learn.

Paired practice is much favoured by those who have succeeded at the highest levels. Before the Olympics, selected helmsmen can be seen practising for five or six hours a day against their reserves. However, to be constructive, it is essential that this form of practice is planned carefully and Chapter 12 goes into this in more detail.

Team and match racing

Team racing and match racing both emphasize tactics and rules. Team racing is the more demanding and complex form of racing, and is therefore better for learning more complex tactical moves and some of the less common rules. But team racing must be between equally matched teams otherwise tactics cease to matter and the better team speeds home ahead of the others. Given close competition it is excellent practice.

Match racing is easier to set up than team racing; it can be included as part of paired practice, which will concentrate more on boat speed and less on tactics. The idea is to sail an agreed match-race course and really use covering tactics and all the other match racing tactics. This is valuable practice for covering and being covered during a proper race.

Both these methods of practice work especially well in a group training programme.

Race post mortem

For the coaching-self the race begins when the boat has crossed the finishing line. Mistakes were made, boats overtook. Why? Can the same problem be avoided next time? Mentally re-running the race is a valuable way of making the most of it and learning from mistakes. Post mortems can be valuable at all levels, and become more and more important as time goes on.

It is the most convenient and easy way to improve and the only certain way of monitoring mistakes. Without post mortem analysis improvement is retarded. To begin with, some will find it difficult, but the technique does provide tremendous benefits and is worth persevering with. It also helps to provide the objectivity which is necessary for successful self-coaching. See Chapter 9.

Visualization is almost an extension of post mortem analysis. The idea is mentally to re-run moments in a race where things went wrong, but in the re-run visualize the moves being correctly done. In other sports this technique has proved as effective as going out and doing the moves for real. Some people find using their imagination in this way a struggle, but they needn't worry. Useful as the technique is, it isn't essential to improvement and can be dropped. Post mortem analysis, though, is vital and ought not to be ignored.

Reading and seeking advice

It's an odd thing about learning anything: you can be told a piece of information, understand what was said, think you know, but really you don't know. Knowing something has to do with experience. You first have to appreciate and digest the piece of knowledge that is being given, then test it to see whether it really works on the water; then you know. Before that you merely carried some factual information in your mind. Anything, to be of value, must be practical. So sailing knowledge truly comes through experience.

Experience can be helped along greatly by other people, either by direct individual help through teaching, or by books. But all the time, the help they give is dependent on your ability to translate what they say into your experience.

That means combining reading with lots of sailing. The two then help each other along. Writers tell us things and we can test the value of what they tell us by trying out their advice on the water. Or, working the other way round, the sailing and racing experience throws up questions which need answering, and we can usually get the answers from books and other sailors. The difficulty is knowing where to find exactly what you need to know without being deluged with a load of stuff which at that moment is irrelevant.

To avoid that it pays to have a relatively small number of books, say ten, which have been selected most carefully. It is always worthwhile asking other people's advice about sailing books, then taking time in the shop to read several sections to see how deeply and clearly they deal with topics you would like to know more about. Be sure too that the author has proved himself on the water, or his advice will be second-rate.

An adequately stocked bookshelf is therefore essential equipment for anyone who is seriously interested in improving his racing. To help stock this bookshelf in Chapter 8, I have selected some of the best books published on racing. Each one deals with a different part of the sport or has a different emphasis. Let us say that starting is one of the three priority areas you're working on; maybe it's been letting you down for some time. Some of the advice you come across in the books is going to give you ideas about altering your starting method for the better. You don't have to agree with what's being said; it's enough for your own thoughts on the problems of starting to be stimulated so that you can find some of the answers you've been looking for.

The booklist I'm recommending can be bought for a fraction of the price of a new suit of sails. New sails might make a difference to your performance or they might not. These books, used in the way suggested, will improve your performance for sure – unless of course you've recently won a Gold medal or World Championship. In which case, congratulations. Otherwise, a shelf loaded with the right books is worth much more than its weight in sailcloth.

Group coaching

Coaching schemes can be extremely helpful, but it is important not to rely too heavily on them for improvement. Everyone's needs are different and a coaching squad tends to be put *en masse* through the same training programme rather than deal with people individually.

Courses that teach racing will usually be most use to someone in the earlier stages of learning to race successfully. Faults are easier for an outsider to recognize at that stage and correct, and towards the back of a fleet there are certain things that everyone will be doing wrong. There is also more to be put right so a good teacher's time is well used. At the higher levels, teaching becomes more difficult as the faults are often subtler and more difficult for an outsider to spot, being fine points of technique or problems of mental approach. Self-coaching is really then the only sure way of improving.

The greatest service any coaching course can provide is to show a sailor how he can teach himself to realize his full sailing potential. In other words it would teach him to teach himself.

Mental fitness

The mental side of racing has a tremendous effect on whether people do well or badly; much more so than is generally realized. A helmsman with the right mental approach can draw on his skills more successfully in a race and will usually beat someone whose mind is not attuned to the job, even if that person has better sailing ability and boat speed. Nor does it matter whether a helmsman's normal position is in the middle of a club fleet or at the top end of a championship fleet, his mental attitudes will make an enormous difference to his performance. Yet few people make any special effort to improve their mental fitness for racing. There are two reasons for this: either they don't know how important it is, or they don't know where to start. Or both.

There are many ways to work on mental fitness. The particular methods you choose must suit your temperament and inclinations. The whole self-coaching approach in itself brings out positive mental attitudes and much of the rest of the book deals with practical ways of improving those attitudes – your belief in your ability, your power of concentration, your ability to handle a crisis, and your power to make the right decisions.

Methods are available to which those who feel the need for profound changes in approach and attitude can turn. These range from spotting negative, performance-damaging attitudes, and controlling thoughts in those areas in a more positive way, to special techniques, some psychological, others meditational. Knowing more about how the mind works when you are out on the water battling for places can itself improve your mental attitudes.

Because the psychological side of sailing has been given so little attention in the past, big differences in helmsmen's performance may be exclusively the result of psychological factors. This is true at all levels but is most noticeable at the top, where years of work have produced highly skilled sailors and the variables between them are on the psychological side.

These are our self-coaching tools. Well used they can transform our sailing for us in a way that over-reliance on racing and old habits can not. In using these methods we need spend no more time sailing, but can use that time more usefully for perfecting the art of racing. How we do that is what the next chapter's about.

6 Making your self-coaching plan

Balance is the essence of a good self-coaching scheme; it must also be enjoyable. It must work on your weak areas so they gradually become stronger. It must fall comfortably into place with the rest of your life – family, work and social life – without pushing things out of balance and so causing emotional problems which will in time affect your sailing. It must not be over ambitious or the effort will be short lived. Steady, sure, long term progress is what you are after and the programme which you set yourself, whether casual or highly disciplined, should be prepared so that you will still be working to it in six months' time.

It must also be flexible enough to leave some freedom of choice about the way things are done. The different ways of learning racing skills are a means to an end, not an end in themselves, and should be used in such a way that you feel right with them. However intently you apply your intellect to preparing a self-coaching programme, it will be no good unless you feel comfortable with it. A good coach gives his pupil some latitude to go his own way and not be straight jacketed into too rigid a method. Even so, self discipline will be necessary early on to get the self-coaching going. Results are never going to come without some effort.

Improvement comes more easily and naturally from a varied and well-balanced approach. Then improvement in one area – say, physical fitness – will help other skills. An unbalanced approach in which one ability is greatly over-emphasized will impede rather than help. Someone who becomes taken up with physical fitness to the point of obsession will damage his light air performance. A helmsman who thinks over much about boat tune will let other racing skills deteriorate, while another who allows tactics to preoccupy him to the exclusion of other facets of racing will find that his boat speed suffers. The answer is therefore steady rather than fanatical improvement and it is important to review the self-coaching plan from time to time to make sure that the learning is well balanced.

There is another kind of balance which it is also as well to be aware of. You learn in two distinct ways: one is by hard conscious effort, the other through a kind of unconscious learning by which a skill comes almost effortlessly. The first is intellectual, the second intuitive. Different skills respond best to different learning methods. Tactics require a very analytical, intellectual approach. Wave technique is all feel and reaction, which is more intuitive. Sailors known as 'naturals' have a strong intuitive feel for the sport. They are even talked about as 'seat of the pants' sailors. You may get some things through the seat of your pants, but logical thought isn't one of them.

Just as there are priorities in what a helmsman might best work on in his sailing abilities, so there are priorities in his selection of learning methods. And time spent in assessing these priorities and applying them to the self-coaching is time very well spent.

For the newcomer to racing and anyone who has not raced for more than two or three seasons, a good grounding in the essential racing skills and an all-round boost in performance is what's required. As my book *Start to Win* was written to help provide just that I can hardly avoid recommending it. The back-of-the-fleet sailor should also miss some races and instead do plenty of solo practice, possibly go on a residential racing course, try some crewing, watch some races and find someone of similar standard to practise against. In the early stages when broad improvement is needed that will provide it. Afterwards self-assessment is necessary to pick out particular weaknesses. Then he can start to work on them.

For the others, the first step is to write down the three chosen weak areas to be worked on. I'll assume, to illustrate the method, that these are: starting; windshifts and heavy weather techniques. The next step is to take each in turn and go through the twelve learning methods and see which might help. It is as well to begin by looking at every possibility and only later drop those which are less valuable or impracticable.

The learning methods (see Chapter 5) are:

race experience
observation
solo practice
crewing
physical fitness
swapping boats and classes
paired practice
team and match racing
post mortems
reading and seeking advice
group coaching
mental fitness

Starting

Now look at each of these in turn and write down all the ways in which you could use these methods to improve starting. Again, write down everything you can think of and sift out what you don't need later.

Race experience Good starting in a race is more difficult than in any of the exercise and practice settings. What's more it happens relatively rarely – once per race (except in the frequent recalls of big championships) – so a lot of racing is good for improving starting. Variety in starting conditions and numbers of starters speeds up improvement, which makes it a good idea to sail in open events and championships away from home.

Observation Watching a keen start can be useful, but don't just watch the start in a general way. Pick out an expert who is starting near your observation position and watch him closely in the final two minutes. See where he positions himself, how fast or slowly he goes and how he puts the power on just before the gun to get himself moving fast off the line in the seconds immediately after the start.

When another class goes off before your own it is always worth taking a good look at their start. It was by doing this that I learned how to make good reaching starts. Brian Heron, many times British Firefly champion, was in the fleet that started ten minutes ahead of us, so I watched him well before the start and especially through the final two minutes. He practised a leeward start in which he reached the wrong way across the line with 50 seconds left, tacked at 26 seconds to go and reached back at speed, hitting the line a second after the gun. This was also how he did it on the start proper. The other 45 boats were almost stationary upwind of him and he took a three length lead before the race was ten seconds old.

Close scrutiny of a preceding start also reveals which end the early leaders come from. That is useful to know, although the knowledge should be treated with some caution – the wind can shift before you get away, and change the pattern.

Solo practice Go out with plastic bottles attached to small weights by thin lines and throw them over the side so they form starting marks. Any floating marks will do but it is as well to have your own. Start by stopping the boat a few feet to leeward of one of the marks, letting the sails out and holding the boat still in the water beside the mark. See how long you can hold in one position until being forced to sheer off one way or the other. Repeat this a few times until it can be done easily and automatically.

Next try reaching up to the mark at speed and stopping dead by slamming the boom out hard and backing the whole mainsail. Do this until you can bring the boat to a halt from full speed in two or three lengths exactly beside the mark. Then try the same thing but approaching the mark at half speed.

After ten or fifteen minutes of this practice begin a series of timed starts. Select the favoured end of the line and aim to start right by the buoy. Set the stop watch exactly as though the practice start was the real one, starting the countdown from three minutes to go. Aim to be going at full speed with the bow just behind the line right at the mark as the crew ends the countdown and calls START. Repeat this half a dozen times. Go for precision starting so that you can hit the right spot at full speed every time. This may not happen for several practice sessions, but that doesn't matter, it will come. When it has, make the practice more difficult by deliberately varying the angle and speed of approach.

Half an hour spent practising in these ways is very good preparation for a real start. Notice that the practice I'm suggesting singles out two basic skills – timing of the final approach and boat control – and, as far as possible, emphasizes the difficulties and then works on them. The other difficulty – dealing with all the other boats – has to be tackled separately, but the solo practice equips you with most of the basics to handle that difficulty much more skilfully and confidently.

These practice sessions should go on regularly once a week until they are no longer necessary. They can then be condensed to five or ten minutes' practice immediately before a race as part of the pre-race warm-up.

Crewing A season's crewing can do wonders for a good helmsman. A crew discovers what it looks and feels like to make a good start and tries to reproduce that when he helms his own boat. He gets used to recognizing those situations in which his helmsman has right of way and those in which he keeps clear. Even the occasional race as a crew can be helpful.

Physical fitness It's mental not physical fitness which counts at the start, and I discuss that below.

Swapping boats and classes Not relevant to this particular skill you are seeking to improve.

Paired practice Go out with someone who wants to do some race training and is of similar standard. Again with the starting marks laid, this time about two boat lengths apart, start and re-start several times, with one of the crews shouting the countdown aloud so it's possible to say whether someone was over the line at the start. Then lay a windward mark and do several starts and beats up to the mark. Vary the starting practice by putting big biases on the line. With a big starboard bias the one who manages to start next to the windward mark at the 'gun' wins the start, which makes for much keener jockeying for position. Finally, lay a very short windward leg and do, say, five races to the weather mark, keeping count of which boat scores most wins. This is a good, competitive practice and tests starting ability as well as can be with just two boats.

Team and match racing These emphasize close tactics, and thus provide excellent practice in starting. Rule knowledge is sharpened up wonderfully – it has to be. In team racing there is the added bonus of critics on your own team who will talk about any serious deficiency in your starting – whether you want them to or not.

Post mortems Mentally re-running starts is the simplest and most convenient method of them all for improving: it can be done anywhere and it really does work. Thinking back over what went right if it was a good start, or wrong if it was not, reinforces good technique and pinpoints mistakes so there is more chance in future starts of making the right moves and less chance of making the wrong ones. Paul Elvström relied heavily on post mortem analysis of races in his early years.

Reading and seeking advice There is no shortage of published material about how to start. Read anything you can find on the subject. Become an expert in the theory; it will help, provided it is combined with plenty of practising and racing. Most important of all, read up the rules. The sections of my own book, *The Rules Book* (Adlard Coles), on the start are designed to answer just those questions that anyone needs to know about the right-of-way before the start. Diagrams show what you can and can't do in those final five minutes. Think up hypothetical situations or think back to knots you got yourself into before starts and work out the rights and wrongs. The IYRU rule book is essential reading and *Elvström Explains the Yacht Racing Rules* (Adlard Coles, 1965) is also very useful.

Talking about starting to someone who outstarts you regularly can be useful, especially if there are specific points you want help on. If someone is consistently better than you at coming out of starts well, they know something or are doing something which you are not, so there is something to learn from them. If you find out from them what it is, you'll become a better sailor. And the club bar is a congenial place in which to improve racing.

Group coaching Starting is a standard exercise in most racing courses. A short line is laid and the fleet put through a sequence of five or six starts, which is particularly good practice because it gets people used to close quarter work with other boats when there's nothing at stake except the start itself.

Mental fitness Some people start badly because they become over-anxious. Others are hesitant about getting involved and battling for position on the line. The over-anxious can calm their anxieties by doing practice starts beforehand. There are also breathing, relaxation, visualization techniques and other methods of preparing mentally. All these topics will be dealt with in detail in later chapters.

The nervous and the battle-shy can begin preparing themselves better by studying the rules. Know your basic rights well enough so that no-one can easily intimidate you. All the other methods of working at starts automatically prepare anyone mentally to start better.

Those are the possibilities. Now you should tailor the list to suit your needs and convenience. Your present standard, the time and effort you are prepared to give, and your preference for particular ways of learning should all now be taken into account, and these will be different for everyone. Convenience is important so straightaway solo practice is in because it is easy to do and particularly useful. Group coaching normally means travelling somewhere to a week-end or week long course, which may not be possible. A coach who comes to the club to take a group is convenient and should not be missed.

Team racing is valuable for improving starting though it is not worth organizing especially for the starting practice it gives. But if team racing does already take place in your club it is worth your while taking part, especially if it will help with other problem areas. (It doesn't particularly help with windshifts or heavy weather technique.)

The thorough way in which you are tackling starting will automatically produce more confidence and more positive attitudes, so that mental fitness can be dropped from most people's lists. Although someone who still wasn't starting well after working for a couple of months in the way I'm suggesting should put mental fitness back on his list. That leaves:

race experience
observation
solo practice
crewing
paired practice

team and match racing
race post mortem
reading and seeking advice

To many all this will be obvious – so obvious in fact that they may not previously have thought of it. It should also be obvious that, properly applied, this self-coaching approach cannot help but improve your starting, almost whatever your present standard. And the amount of extra time required to achieve that improvement need be no more than half an hour a week.

Windshifts

The second item on the list for working on is windshifts. Some sailors can read and use windshifts almost infallibly; others can't see them at all. It is partially a knack, something akin to being good at catching a ball, a gift which some people just have, but it is also an ability which can be learned, and anyone can use self-coaching to show themselves exactly how to spot windshifts and how to use them as well as the best.

I will assume windshift blindness and show, as with starting, how to take this one ability and develop it to a high degree. We begin, as before, by looking at all the learning methods in turn.

Racing For a helmsman who usually sails in the middle or back of a twenty boat club fleet, racing is only moderate practice for spotting and learning about windshifts. Boats ahead churn up the wind, making the shifts less obvious, and in addition, nearby boats are such a distraction that it is difficult to settle down and tune in to the shifts. The front of a fleet on the other hand provides very good practice in windshift working. So unless a middle- or back-of-the-fleet helmsman uses other methods than racing for learning about windshifts, he is trapped and will learn either very slowly or not at all. The answer is to use a mix of methods which includes racing.

Observation The time to watch is on a blustery day when the wind is off the land and shifting a lot; watching can then be very instructive. Mainly it shows how much is lost by helmsmen who take wrong shifts. You will see boats being headed 15° and continuing on the same tack, while another boat tacks and a minute later has come from twenty yards behind to thirty yards ahead. But make sure that such a gain has, in fact, been caused by tacking on a header, and not by going back into a more favourable tidal current while the others carried on out into an adverse tide.

This type of place changing due to windshifts happens much of the time. During a race you may not see why it is happening since there is so much going on in your own boat and immediately around it, but without all that distraction you can watch how a shifting wind changes the order throughout a fleet.

The best place from which to see all this happening is above. Bassenthwaite Lake in the Lake District is surrounded by mountains and from one of these mountainsides a race can be seen unfolding like a game of chess. Gusts are visible on the lake's surface before they reach groups of boats. Those crews who are too preoccupied with other things either to notice or make use of a heading shift when it comes can be seen sailing off at what looks from above, and is, a disastrously wrong direction. Others, who take the right shifts can be seen clawing their way up through the fleet. There the shifts are big – up to 20° in a fairly stable wind – but the effects of even 10° shifts are easily recognized from a shore or rescue boat. Paleston cliffs and the headland at the south of Falmouth are two other good high vantage points where championships often take place.

Solo practice Anyone who has difficulty spotting windshifts can learn the art in an hour or two's intensive solo practice. Those who are weak on shifts, who spot some and miss others, can become much sharper at spotting them by this type of practice.

As with starting, the plan is to isolate the problem, and then tackle it on its own without complications and distractions. When you get windshifts on their own they stand less chance of bemusing you as they might in a race; mastering them is only a matter of time and some effort. And that time is best spent to begin with in sailing long legs close-hauled – very precisely close-hauled too, with the jib just on the point of lifting all the time. Most back-of-the-fleet sailors tend to sail continuously 5° below the point where the jib luffs. This is no good for windward speed and no good for windshift spotting; the wind can head 5° and the helmsman won't know. But sail constantly on the edge of the wind on flattish water and the jib will partially back when the 5° header comes. On these long tacks the helmsman should continually check his angle against the shore when there is one dead ahead. He should also keep glancing at his compass (a good sized compass too, not one two inches across which is only of use for finding the way home in fog).

As soon as you can consistently spot these small variations in wind direction you should begin to tack on the heading shifts. Every time the wind shifts to make the boat bear away you tack, which means that the boat travels less distance through the water to the weather mark. (Reading about shifts will give a full explanation of the theory of windshift tactics.)

Often the wind bends round bays and these bends can be recognized by sailing long legs close-hauled. The course gradually alters as the boat sails its long leg. Bends can also be recognized by sailing on a dead run and taking regular direction checks against the shore or taking compass readings.

With regular weekly practice windshift spotting becomes second nature, and awareness of which is the favoured tack will remain, even in the middle of a sizeable fleet. But accurate and sensitive perception of windshifts does take time to develop; it doesn't come in just one practice session. If it isn't coming after three or four sessions, it's probably because you are not sailing the boat accurately enough to windward with the jib always on the point of lifting.

Crewing As a crew it is easy to see a helmsman's good moves and his mistakes. In a season's crewing for a successful helmsman, learning about windshifts will happen almost automatically, although it can be speeded up by reading and doing some helming, not necessarily in races. Even the occasional race as a crew can be instructive – the sharp end of the boat is a very good place from which to watch a race.

Physical fitness This will not help with this skill.

Swapping classes One design classes are far better than restricted and handicap classes for learning about windshifts. In a one design like the Laser the boats around you are all going at about the same speed so that one tack sailed in a wrong shift means lost places. In a restricted fleet a faster boat going off on a wrong shift might still gain by sheer boat speed and the effect of the windshift can go unnoticed. In one design racing, windshifts therefore play a more obvious part in the racing, and the simpler the one design the better. Regular racing in a class like the Laser, Firefly or Sunfish is excellent for teaching awareness and use of windshifts.

Paired practice This too is excellent for acquiring a good feel for windshifts. Paired practice also shows up the big gains and losses that can be made by working the shifts well or badly. Both helmsmen must be of similar standard for the practice to be really effective. The idea is to race together, one shaving the other's stern as the two boats start on opposite tacks, but not sail as in a normal match race where the emphasis is on covering and tacking. The plan is rather to avoid tacking on each other's wind so that sailing speed and good use of the shifts become the race-winning factors. This is a very important point because if, instead of avoiding each other's wind, the helmsmen start covering each other, windshifts become irrelevant – even the big ones.

When practising a particular ability the type of practice should always be arranged to develop that ability, not others which the helmsman may already be good at. Paired practice done in this way is one of the best and most enjoyable ways of really getting the hang of windshifts.

Team and match racing This will not really help with an improvement in spotting windshifts.

Post mortem analysis A particularly good memory is needed to recall every detail of a race and that can take seasons to develop. There may be whole legs which have left little impression on the memory, while those incidents which can be remembered are too vague to be of any use for post mortem analysis. Like everything else, it's all a question of practice. Make some effort to remember races and memory improves: details become clearer and, if there was some awareness of windshifts during the race, these shifts and their effects can be recalled.

Post mortem analysis of windshifts can be useful for seeing how places were won or lost by good or bad use of shifts Understanding what went wrong, and why, doesn't ensure that the same thing won't happen again, but it does reduce the odds on future mistakes. Big windshifts where the wind swings round one way over several minutes, or where it blows in a steady curve all afternoon, are well worth analysis afterwards. 'How could I have foreseen that? Were there any signs or clues which I could look for in future races?' These are the kinds of questions to ask and find answers to.

Reading The most important point books make about windshifts is that if a helmsman doesn't know much about them he can forget about winning many races. There is a good deal of knowledge that can be learned from books and magazine articles. These published insights into the secret habits of a wind bend, an offshore wind, a wind blowing down an estuary, thermal winds and sea breezes are very handy to know. Knowing the theory can speed up the learning appreciably, since what seemed random events during races often turn out to be part of a pattern, and therefore predictable. And once you can predict what the wind is likely to do you are one step nearer to sailing the flawless race.

Seeking advice Specific questions put to someone who is particularly good in a shifting wind produce specific answers. Local knowledge can be picked up in this way. With the wind in a particular direction it will often pay to sail more to one side of a beat or approach a mark from a particular side. The club expert will know this, which is partly why he's the club expert. Ask him and he'll probably tell you. At national and international level the expert may not prove so helpful. If he tells you at all he might just tell you the opposite, although if you openly and straightforwardly ask what you want to know, the top level helmsman will usually give a straight answer, and you'll learn something.

Group coaching This may not be specifically useful.

Mental fitness If you are relaxed and concentrating you will be more responsive to changing conditions.

Before we look at how all these different ways of learning about starting and windshifts might be put together in a self-coaching timetable, we should look at how best to strengthen heavy weather sailing. This time I am not going to spell out the method but leave you to work it out for yourself, as you would on any of the other fifty or more problem areas you might at some time want to work on.

7 Survival racing

Heavy weather sailing is something you grow into when you have been racing for some time, but you can very much speed up the process of mastering heavy weather if you go about it the right way. So much of the ability is feel and balance that no amount of knowledge will help a helmsman who doesn't get thoroughly used to force five and six so that he is fully controlling the boat rather than being controlled by it. That means going out sometimes in really heavy weather just for the fun of it, even if it's necessary to reef to stay upright.

When you can do that you are most of the way there; then you need more detailed knowledge of just what to do to go as fast as possible when it's really blowing. Some of this information will be found in books, some of it will be picked up by trial and error, some of it can be learned by closely watching some heavy weather races, and some can be learned by asking people who have mastered the art.

I am writing about smaller boats since that is where my main experience lies, but the principles and techniques are much the same for larger keel boats. The fastest way to learn to helm a 50-footer successfully is to spend a season or two in a dinghy learning to do well in that, as many dinghy champions have shown when they've been given the helm of Admiral's Cup yachts. So when the keel boat man reads how to avoid capsizes, he should think in terms of being overpowered and slowed, broached or otherwise flattened.

Heavy weather fear

The one essential of successful heavy weather racing is fearlessness. A helmsman or crew who get rid of fear or excessive anxiety automatically start thinking about getting round the course as fast as possible. But if they sail tensed up through fear of a capsize, knock-down, gear failure or are plagued by a general, irrational fear of heavy weather, their whole approach to the sailing becomes half-hearted and tentative.

Heavy weather panic is by no means rare and it afflicts the big, athletic and strong, not just the timid or the physically less strong. Nor does it seem related necessarily to courage in other fields. I was once talking to a keen Laser sailor who had taken up the sport six months earlier. The club race was due to start and the wind was blowing force three, maybe just touching four. Yet this helmsman didn't seem in the least keen to go out, which was odd, so I asked whether he was racing.

'No, I don't think so,' was the uneasy reply.

'Why not?'

'Well last week it was blowing force five and the boat took over. I couldn't control it downwind and I must have capsized a dozen times. I've rather lost my confidence.'

'Come on,' I urged him, 'it's hardly more than force three out there.'

'I know,' he replied, 'but last week I really scared myself. In my previous sport I never got that scared.'

'What sport was that?' I inquired innocently.

'Motor racing.'

In time he regained his confidence and was able to remove some of his heavy weather fear, but I didn't manage to persuade him out that afternoon. This kind of fear is nothing to be ashamed of or unduly worried about, and someone who squarely accepts the fact that they have a problem about getting frightened in a blow is half way to conquering it.

One way to go about fully resolving the problem is to go out in a good breeze and deliberately capsize many times. By doing that you discover that there is really nothing to be frightened of, but it is important not to do this practice in too strong a wind or there may be trouble getting back to the club or recovering from capsizes. Fatigue could then set in and, instead of removing the heavy weather fear, it could become more deep rooted. But in moderate conditions deliberate capsizes will help most people. If that doesn't work or is only partially successful, longer term methods may be necessary and these are dealt with in later chapters about mental fitness.

Good control in heavy weather requires strength and physical fitness. Regular sailing is sufficient to give club sailors an adequate level of fitness, but for the ambitious sailor, some jogging and gymnasium exercising will give greater physical ability and therefore greater control when it is really blowing. It will also enable him to keep going flat out when others are tiring, for when we start to tire we lose some of our control over the boat.

High speed survival upwind

The first essential for success in survival conditions is to get round the course without capsizing. That in itself in force six or seven (and for some force four or five) is quite an achievement. Succeed in staying upright in such extreme conditions and you'll automatically finish well placed. And to know how to stay upright in 25 knots of wind you first have to know what makes you capsize, so let's look at the more popular ways of capsizing.

When beating in force six or seven gusts the knockdown is probably the most widely favoured type of capsize with the middle and back of the fleet sailors. A helmsman and crew may believe that survival in a sudden force six gust is impossible and nothing they could do would save a capsize. They would be wrong. Any centreboard dinghy properly sailed will survive a force six gust on the beat. Most will survive a force seven gust and some will even stand up to force eight. It all depends on how the boat is handled.

Knockdown capsizes on the beat usually happen because the jib is cleated board tight and the helmsman spills wind by completely letting go the mainsheet. In moderate winds you won't capsize this way, but given enough wind this is a sure way to go in. The jib pushes the bow off and, with no mainsail to balance the helm, the boat develops excessive lee helm and nothing you do with the rudder will bring her back up to a close-hauled course. The result is that she is forced beam on to the wind, forward way is lost because the jib stalls and the whole mainsail flogs uselessly. With the jib square on to the wind and the enormous drag of a flogging mainsail, the capsizing moment of the rig becomes greater than the righting moment of the fully extended weight of helmsman and crew.

This type of capsize can quite easily be avoided. In the first place, if the boat were kept approximately on close-hauled course and not allowed to lose way and fall beam on to the wind, excessive capsizing forces would not develop. So by sailing with the jib eased so that both jib and mainsail spill air, lee helm will not then develop; nor will the full area of a stalled jib be presented to the wind if the boat does fall much below a close-hauled course. Not only will the boat survive the gust with the jib eased, but she'll be surviving with even greater boat speed than before the gust arrived.

By spilling on the jib and main together it is possible to stay upright until the wind is so strong that, with both mainsail and jib flogging, the heeling moment of the rig finally exceeds the righting moment of the fully extended helmsman and crew. For most dinghies that only happens in force eight or more.

When the conditions are so strong that the jib has to be eased, it still pays to sail to windward pinching with the jib lifting several inches back from the luff. The mainsail too should be eased so that the first third or so is backwinding. The boat is then balanced on the helm and can be feathered to windward in such a way that the heeling moment of the rig always balances the crew weight.

In the heaviest weather the boat is feathered higher on the wind, so that even half the jib and half the mainsail are backwinding; in less extreme wind the boat can be driven off with the whole jib and most of the mainsail drawing. Heavy weather sailing is a balancing act – the art is to use your sense of balance and feel to keep the heeling forces of the rig and righting moment of the crew weight in equilibrium.

The way to improve this sense of balance and feel is, as I said earlier, to sail for fun in heavy weather both in and out of races. But you can work more directly still. Rudderless sailing is an excellent way to acquire this sense of balance and feel quickly – you have to or you fall in. This type of practice is best tried in medium weather to begin with until the boat can be fully controlled without its rudder. For the more advanced sailors, sailing trapeze boats single handed from the trapeze without a rudder is excellent practice. When you can do that you really know boat control.

Big gusts cause most trouble, but a capsize can usually be avoided by spotting them before they arrive. Fortunately you can't mistake the darker and more threatening-looking patches of water that they send out as visiting cards. All you need do to predict their arrival is to keep glancing upwind every twenty seconds at the surface of the water.

With practice you should be able to read the water well enough to predict to the second the moment the full force of the gust will strike, which will enable you to ease the jib and sit out fully *before* the gust strikes. Then the first impact of the gust drives the boat forwards rather than sideways, or even, horizontal.

The aim when sailing a dinghy to windward in heavy weather should always be to sail dead upright. Get maximum crew weight over the side to achieve that, otherwise you will need to sacrifice extra sail power to compensate for lack of sitting out moment. But once you have your crew and yourself sitting out to the limit, the boat must not be allowed to heel, whatever it takes to achieve that – including spilling wind from most of the mainsail and most of the jib. Keep the boat dead level and you'll have more control, more speed and a higher finishing position.

Upright sailing skills are dealt with in an earlier chapter so we shan't go through the practising methods again here. Nevertheless they are extremely valuable and anyone wanting to work at their heavy weather sailing would do well to use the windward heeling practice recommended earlier.

Lifting the centreboard a third of the way will make most dinghies easier to hold up on the beat in the heaviest weather, though leeway is increased. By sailing with two-thirds plate the heeling moment of the boat is decreased because the centre of the lateral resistance of the hull (CLR) is raised closer to the centre of the sideways (heeling) forces or effort of the rig (CE). This brings a significant reduction in the heeling tendency of the boat, so that less spilling of wind is necessary.

The risk of being blown flat is also reduced, because as the boat heels even more of the centreboard comes out of the water and the hull will slide off to leeward rather than capsize. Some classes actually sail faster to windward in very heavy weather with the plate partially raised – a secondary benefit is movement aft of the CLR in relation to the CE, thus cutting down any tendency to weather helm.

There is a temptation to relax and sit in as soon as the boat becomes level. Don't – that's just the time your sitting out provides the biggest righting moment. I always aim to sail upwind heeled slightly to windward and fail by just enough to leave the boat plumb upright most of the time.

Provided you and your crew are sitting out hard and spilling and feathering up to windward as much as necessary to keep the boat upright, good windward speed is an automatic result. You will also have an easier and faster ride as a gust strikes, even if you didn't spot it coming. With the boat sailing level and crew weight right over the side, the wind has much more to do to heel the boat; it has to lift you and your crew several feet into the air. As this begins to happen you have time to ease the mainsheet and pinch up before the boat heels unduly. But when helmsman and crew are not sitting out hard nor holding the boat level before the gust, the first response has to be to get their weight properly over the side. While they are managing that the boat heels too far and the opportunity for playing the mainsheet and helm for maximum boat speed is lost. Instead they flounder sideways at reduced speed until control is regained or they swim. It is a mistake to sit out hard *only* when things are going wrong, not when they're going right.

Many people have the idea that spilling wind is bad because it's sacrificing power. In fact much more power is lost in a dinghy by allowing the boat to heel. Spilling wind from the mainsail and, when conditions get really heavy, from the jib gets rid of excessive and unmanageable heeling or leeward forces in the rig, yet retains the essential forward driving forces. The result: good forward speed without excessive heeling or leeway.

The penalties for heeling in a blow are:

Weather helm develops This happens mainly because the forward driving force of the rig is no longer over the centreline but acting from over the water several feet to leeward. To counteract the tendency that this creates for the boat to screw up into wind, the helmsman hauls his tiller up to windward and the angled rudder acts as a brake, producing several times as much drag as a straight rudder.

The rig loses power It is often forgotten that the rig becomes appreciably less efficient as it heels, turning more of the forces available for forward motion into the downward acting force already mentioned. Even with 15° of heel there is a fraction less power available to convert into forward motion than when the rig is upright. As the boat heels to over 25° and more the power falls off dramatically.

Leeway increases Even at 10° of heel leeway increases slightly. At 20° or 25° leeway increases considerably in dinghies, and leeway becomes excessive when this heeling combined with loss of speed causes the centreboard to stall. This happens particularly easily on boats with fairly small, narrow boards.

Crew weight becomes less effective When the boat heels, the centres of gravity of the hiking helmsman and trapezing crew move closer to the centre of buoyancy of the hull, and thus transmit less righting moment to the rig than when upright. Also, as the crew and helmsman are lifted higher above the water, their bodies come into a faster windstream so drag is marginally increased.

Knowing all this will sharpen up our powers of observation when we go out and watch a race – you will see more because you know what to look for. Learning takes place in many ways, and one kind of learning helps another along. Reading and learning more about the theory helps you to understand and see how you should be doing things. Observing a race helps you to understand the theory by seeing the practical side of it in operation.

There is one technique which can work really well for holding the boat flat as a gust first strikes without sacrificing unnecessary power. At the moment of the gust's initial impact the helmsman lets go an arm's length of sheet and *immediately* pulls most of it back in again, at the same time pushing the helm to leeward to keep the boat pointing up. If the boat still wants to heel, he again lets out an arm's length of sheet and sheets back in. He may have to pump the mainsail in this way two or three times, before the boat is properly under control on a fairly high-pointing close-hauled course moving fast.

The purpose of this mainsail pumping is two-fold. Letting out the mainsail as the gust strikes allows the initial blast to pass without heeling the boat unduly. Immediately hauling in most of the released sheet fills the aft part of the mainsail and, acting like an airborne rudder, holds the boat on a close-hauled course. Two or three repeated pumps of the mainsheet allow the helmsman to hold the boat level and on a high close-hauled course until the main impact of the gust has passed. The technique is particularly useful in a sudden lifting gust.

It is usually better to over prepare for an imminent gust than to be caught unawares. If the jib has been eased too much, it can easily be sheeted in right away with little ground lost. Near a windward shore in blustery weather the gusts tend to be more vicious, more variable in direction and shorter lived. In these conditions it usually pays to sail with the jib uncleated, or at least freed off a few inches.

At the back end of a gust an extra kick of speed can be picked up by remaining sitting out hard a moment longer than you think you should, at the same time sheeting the mainsail back in to its usual, more central, close-hauled position. This gives an extra two or three feet gain after the gust has gone. Repeated after each gust, these small gains become boat lengths and places by the end of the windward leg.

The gains at the end of each gust by doing this aren't too easy to see during a race when there's so much going on, so it's difficult to know initially whether you are doing the technique properly. One way to find out is to practise with one other boat. The pair of you sail up the beat staying close together, though not in each other's wind, taking long tacks. Each time a gust comes and passes on, you have a yardstick to see how well you handled it. And before too long you'll be able to recognize that little boost which comes from handling the end of the gust correctly. How you get on in the first part of the gust will be obvious anyway, but doing this paired practice gives better incentive for improvement than practising alone. Paired practice is unnecessary in the early stages, but once the gust handling ability is well developed it is the best way to develop it further.

A gusty wind has up its sleeve one devastating trump card: the slam header – the sharp gust that attacks suddenly from ahead, backing the jib and tipping you in to windward. Everyone knows that this can happen, but the middle- and back-of-the-fleet helmsman and crew tend to sail gusty, heavy weather beats as though it's always going to happen. They shouldn't be so worried. A slam header violent enough to make a capsize certain is extremely rare. I can remember only one in all my racing and that was when beating in the lee of a mountain in an unusually fluky force six. The fear of the slam header has a far more devastating effect on people's heavy weather windward sailing than the thing itself.

Curiously, helmsman and crew who don't sit out hard when

beating in a gusty wind make themselves more vulnerable, not less, to the sudden violent header. Dinghies have one thing in common with bicycles – they tend to be more easily controlled and kept upright when travelling fast. If you fail to drive your boat hard upwind she goes more slowly and does not respond as positively to rudder movements. When you do work hard the boat is more responsive and will bear off more sharply as the header strikes.

The state of extra alertness and agility which helmsmen and crews enter into when sailing hard means that their own response to the slam header is faster, more definite and therefore more effective. An alert crew can be sitting out hard one moment and the next be diving for the lee side of the boat with the jib already uncleated. A crew whose sitting out efforts were tentative in the first place tends to react tentatively to the slam header. A keenly aware helmsman working his boat to windward for all he's worth will bear off faster and more positively than one who is sailing over-cautiously.

Most significantly, a really perceptive helmsman and crew will know that a slam header is coming *before* it arrives; it will not catch them unawares. Close scrutiny of the water upwind will tell them when a gust is about to arrive and the direction of the wind in that gust.

In shifty wind a top-flight helmsman will be doing a continual read-out of the water immediately upwind so that he not only adjusts his mainsheet, but alters his boat direction to anticipate any gusts. This naturally helps his survival on a brisk beat, but it also enables him to sail more confidently and faster than those whose only clues to windstrength and direction are the wind indicators and sails. Boats ahead are also excellent wind direction indicators. Many a windward capsize has been a warning to a boat behind to prepare for a slam header.

One of the all-time favourite ways of capsizing, and as widely used today as when the jamb cleat was invented, is the backed-jib tack. The crew fails to uncleat the jib during the tack so that once past head to wind the boat is flipped in by the backed jib. In survival conditions even uncleating the jib requires a determined effort.

The heaviest gusts make tacking hazardous. The enormous drag of the flogging sails as the boat goes head to wind may be powerful enough to stop the boat dead in the water and throw her rapidly into reverse – that is, into irons. Always look for lulls to tack in, and always go into a tack with good boat speed, determined to get round onto the new board. It's the tentative or half-hearted attempt that puts the boat into irons.

Here again you can improve faster outside races by practising. To begin with practise tacking in the lulls until you can handle that well, than graduate to the gusts. In that way you come to terms with tacking in stronger wind than you would usually choose during a race, for then you would go in the lulls, not the gusts. By making the problem even more difficult in practice sessions, tacking during a heavy weather race becomes so much easier and more fluent.

Another way of learning about heavy weather is to crew for someone who has mastered it. Not only do you learn some of the tricks I've mentioned (some of which I learned myself by crewing), but you know what the boat looks and feels like when the helmsman is in control, and what it looks and feels like when he's not. And when you resume helming you have that memory of how it should be done to help you along.

The one thing that is essential with heavy weather beats is to attack them with determination and drive the boat hard. Not only does that make staying upright more likely but it's the right attitude for getting to the weather mark first. And when you do capsize, work out why. Except in the most extreme heavy weather, a capsize is always your own fault, never the wind's.

Downwind

The worst problems my motor-racing Laser friend experienced were when he went onto a dead run. The boat took control and he became little more than a helpless and very alarmed passenger. Most of the capsizes happened when the boat sheered off suddenly to leeward and the rig fell smartly to windward. He retired from the race after failing to find any way of preventing these windward capsizes.

Certainly, running in heavy weather takes courage. Once you're pointing dead downwind you move fast, whether you want to or not. And unlike a beam reach, which allows you to ease off the mainsail and spill wind, a run provides no safety valve which will slow you down or get you out of trouble. With the boat powering off on a fast plane and a force six wind dead astern, survival is almost everything. Speed, maybe more of it than you'd like, is inevitable; survival is not.

So what can be done to be sure of staying upright in such conditions? The first step is to learn what causes the capsize. If you know that you know what danger signs to look out for and so can avoid doing anything that might put you in. Let's start by analysing the causes of my fellow Laser sailor's windward capsizes.

The most likely problem was that he was letting the mainsail out too far. A Laser, like a Finn, has no shrouds to prevent the sail being let out beyond a right angle to the boat's centreline. When the sail is let out beyond a certain point the direction of the air flow over it reverses: the flow tends to be from the mast towards the leech, rather than from leech to luff as it would be with the boom sheeted further in.

This reversal of flow reverses the direction of the rig's heeling forces. Instead of there being a leeward heeling force, the reverse flow generates a windward heeling force. With the helmsman already on the windward side, the windward heeling force in the rig makes a death roll to windward inevitable and quick. It can be avoided by keeping the mainsail further in. Then the windward heeling moment created by the helmsman sitting to windward can be counterbalanced by the leeward heeling moment of the rig.

Another, though more precarious, way to prevent a windward capsize is for the helmsman to sit to leeward with the boom sheeted just forward of square, and to run by the lee. In some single handed boats – the Laser among them – a little extra power is available from the rig when doing this. However, the boat is then more difficult to keep upright so this is not something to try in survival conditions.

One Laser sailor discovered this technique by accident. He bore off to gybe at the start of a heavy weather run, moved his weight over before the boom came across but failed to make the gybe happen. Afraid of doing anything drastic to induce the gybe, he remained for the rest of the run sitting on the 'wrong' side of the boat running precariously by the lee at enormous speed. The gains he had inadvertently made were enough to encourage him to sail his runs that way deliberately when conditions were right.

One sure way to make any boat without a spinnaker uncontrollable on a heavy weather run is to sail with too slack a kicking strap. To control the boat on the run you must have the kicker tight enough to prevent the top of the sail twisting off forward when either a gust strikes or the boat buries its bow into the back of wave. And that is very tight indeed.

With a half-tightened kicker, the first impact of a gust twists the sail so that the top third is pushed forward of square. The windflow reverses over this upper part of the sail and again you have windward heeling forces. The boat reacts with a sudden lurch to windward, which is usually violent enough to put the boat out of the helmsman's control and into a death roll to windward. Everyone gets very wet.

A spinnaker makes staying upright on the run easier. Set fairly high, the sail creates a downdraught. This produces a lifting force in the sail which hoists the bow over the backs of waves so the hull is more easily driven, especially in the gusts. The other big benefit of the spinnaker is that it makes the boat plane faster, which reduces the apparent wind and the heeling forces in the rig, making the boat more stable.

Although a dead run turns into a relatively secure ride with a spinnaker up, the risk of capsize increases dramatically when hoisting and lowering it. A cool helmsman and sure-footed, fast-moving crew can nevertheless set spinnakers safely in near-survival weather.

During the hoist the helmsman should move right aft to counterbalance the crew moving forward to fix the spinnaker pole. The boat should be kept on a dead run since most capsizes happen at this time because the boat is allowed to head up and broach.

Even with the spinnaker up and drawing well, there is still a possibility of broaching. The broach usually happens because the helmsman is too slow on the helm to counter the broach early. A broach starts as a fairly small luff. Catch the luff in time and get the boat bearing off back onto a dead run, then there's no broach and no capsize.

Windward capsizes under spinnaker happen because the guy and pole are hauled too far aft while the sheet is eased too much. Instead of being presented square to the wind, inducing a vertical downdraught, the sail is now angled so that the wind also flows horizontally – from the luff of the spinnaker to the leech. This horizontal flow generates a heeling force acting to windward, which in moderate wind may not appear to matter (though the spinnaker will be less efficient). But when a gust arrives the heeling force will increase sharply, contributing both to the entertainment of spectators and the livelihood of yachting photographers.

Without a spinnaker a boat running is more stable with the jib goose-winged than with it left to look after itself in the lee of the mainsail. The goose-winged jib balances the rig and, like the spinnaker, gives that extra lift and forward drive which helps to prevent the bow burying in the biggest gusts.

For both survival and speed on heavy weather runs it is important to get helmsman and crew weight as far back as possible, one on each side of the boat. Without a spinnaker the boat becomes hydrodynamically unstable in the heaviest gusts because the mainsail presses the bow down, tilting the hull forward onto the narrower forward sections and lifting the wider and flatter aft part of the hull off the water. Get the hull riding on these flatter aft sections by moving weight right back and the boat has much greater stability. Not only that, she'll go faster.

Keeping the crew weight right aft also reduces the chances of getting into the familiar downwind roll – a rhythmic and ever-increasing roll from side to side which usually ends with a splash. The way to stop the roll ever happening is to sheet in the mainsheet several feet so the boom is 15 or 20° aft of a right angle to the centreline.

Once the roll has begun it becomes self-perpetuating because, as the rig sways from side to side, the air flow over the surface of the mainsail reverses with each oscillation. When the rig rocks to windward the air flow over the mainsail is to leeward, and it reverses as the rig rocks back to leeward. But by sheeting in the mainsail so the boom is a foot or two off the lee shroud, the flow over the sail is always from leech to luff, never from luff to leech. The boat will then have greater stability and any roll which begins will be damped rather than amplified by the rig.

So the most secure way to sail a survival run without spinnaker is for the helmsman to sit firmly on the windward side deck with the crew wedged just to leeward of the centreline, both well aft. With the mainsail sheeted in slightly from square, the rig's heeling moment is counterbalanced by the combined weight of the helmsman and crew being to windward. Any tendency to heel can then be counteracted entirely by rudder movements. The boat will be moving fast, and quick jabs of the rudder are very effective for killing any tendency to heel or to damp a rhythmic roll.

It's important for helmsman and crew to stay firmly rooted by their backsides to the boat; they then become part of the boat, doubling its moment of inertia and greatly slowing down any rolling there may be. The certain way to turn a rhythmic roll into a quick capsize is for helmsman and crew to get onto their feet and attempt a corrective dance. Only when the boat heels more than about 25° on a dead run should anyone move position. The movement should be small and the one to move is the crew.

With practice a dead run need be no more scarey than any other point of heavy weather sailing. You know you've got it right when, with weight right aft, the boat can find no other way to put you in except by cartwheeling forwards. Rare as this is, it happened to a friend of mine in a Fireball on a day when racing was cancelled. As he hit the water he cut his face on the masthead wind indicator – a war wound to be proud of.

In this section ten of the twelve learning methods have been used. The more angles you attack the problem from the less of a problem it becomes and the more thoroughly you solve it. Borrowing a different class of boat, more sensitive to weight and livelier than your own would be another way to improve these skills. That, like crewing, might be difficult to arrange, but if it were easy to find yourself a temporary crewing job with a champion or swap classes with someone else in your club you would learn something. Even so, no one method is indispensable and the other nine will show you all we need to know if we apply them to our heavy weather sailing over several weeks and months. Big improvements would then be an inevitable result of the effort we were putting in.

Quite deliberately, I have gone much more deeply into the learning process than many will need for their own sailing, but for the purposes of our self-coaching it is good to know what the possibilities are, to know exactly what can be done if you put your mind to it and how it can be done. From that you can take as much as you need to improve your heavy weather ability and leave the rest.

8 Researching success

Now that the self-coaching method is clear some of the areas which have so far only been sketched in can be expanded. One of these, an important one too, is researching success – discovering exactly what does make the best helmsmen win: the fine points of detail in their racing technique, boat tuning and tactical abilities which take them right to the front.

Most people when applying themselves to winning do not apply themselves properly to this research. It is complementary to self-assessment, only instead of looking at yourself to see what you are doing wrong, you study what the best helmsmen do that is so right, then learn more exactly what you are self-coaching yourself towards.

One reason why so many make a half-hearted job of researching success is that they haven't thought out just how important this research is. They say to themselves 'To get higher up the fleet I just have to sail better,' without really asking what 'better' is. And it is as I've said before, doing all the detailed tasks of racing which are involved in sailing a boat efficiently round the course more perfectly than those he beats. Researching success is defining in detail, what those tasks are and how the champion is doing them; it is a matter of getting right to the bottom of the question, 'What is better?'

There are several ways of researching what a sailor does to get himself round the course fast. These ways are:

Reading books and articles by champions. Lectures and films can also be very useful.

Observing how the expert sails; watching for the details, the things he does and you don't.

Being coached by someone who knows more than you.

Seeking advice from an expert, even asking to measure up his boat, rig and sheet positions.

Crewing to find out how a top helmsman operates.

Swapping classes teaches skills and techniques which are particularly important in one class but apply to all.

Trial and error is the only way left for the champion, but it can also be a valuable way for anyone to learn what works and what doesn't.

Other spheres. On the psychological side much more understanding has been gained in other sports and activities than in sailing. The same is true in preparing the body for competition.

The best methods to use to research success depend on a helmsman's present needs, and therefore his general standard. All of them will work at any level, but the nearer the top of his class a helmsman is the more he must rely on observation, trial and error and drawing on experience in other spheres. When he is right at the top his research must mainly be through experiment – systematic trial and error during paired practice with someone of near-equal standard. A very good coach could also help him, but at the top level improvement is harder to come by – there is no-one doing it better from whom to learn.

At all other levels researching success is easy, provided the effort is made to do it at all. A helmsman must want to do it, for not all do; some are more comfortable a little way down a fleet than at the front. In spite of what they may say, they don't really want to win. They see themselves as inferior to the people who are winning, and since they don't see themselves as winners, they are reluctant to take the necessary steps to become winners. However, those who so devote themselves to losing that they inadvertently capsize or hit marks when in the lead, or otherwise resort to pieces of seeming incompetence in their pursuit of failure, are in a minority. Most who are prone to 'bad luck' of this sort are not aware that the real reason is an unconscious fear of winning, but even they would get more out of the sport if they were able to do what they will tell you they want to do – win. Which of course, means doing all the detailed tasks of sailing a race better than they are doing them at present.

Reading

One of the best ways of finding out what these details are is to read up what the experts say. The first difficulty here is to know what to read. Far more has been written than should have been so I will give a brief résumé of some of the best books at present available.

For basic sailing skills the back-of-the-fleet sailor can do no better than read Richard Creagh-Osborne's *This is Sailing* (Nautical Macmillan, 1970). It is clear, beautifully illustrated, and very basic. The follow-on from that is my book *Start to Win* (Adlard Coles 1975) which stops short of the highest level but unlike other books on learning to race, does make clear the things that matter most to the middle-of-the-fleet sailor in his quest for first place, explaining them as clearly and logically as the author can manage. Some books by the world's best sailors, on the other hand, tend to say what matters to them in winning races rather than what is important to the club sailor – two very different things. For example they will take it for granted that the reader can spot and use windshifts and that he understands all the basic requirements of good starting, so the author might devote pages to the merits of swinging spreaders or the importance of diet. Interesting, but not much use to the club sailor who falls in every time the wind blows and doesn't even know the right angle to sheet his mainsail. As a helmsman's standard improves so the advice of these top level helmsmen becomes more relevant. *Sailing from Start to Finish* by Yves-Louis Pinaud (Adlard Coles, 1975) and *This is Racing* (Nautical Macmillan, 1972) by Richard Creagh-Osborne also provide good information for the club sailor.

The most authoritative and readable book on more involved tactics is Stuart Walker's *Advanced Racing Tactics* (Angus and Robertson, 1976). Not a beginner's book, but for the aspiring club or world champion it is required reading. The author analyses his own races, first setting the scene and telling the story of a race, often in some championship, and afterwards analysing the correct moves and the wrong ones. He chooses each race to illustrate a particular problem so that a wide range of tactics is covered as, to a lesser extent, are psychological attitudes. By reading the book you can learn through Stuart Walker's mistakes (or more often those of his opponents). The book has already established itself as a classic.

There are two books which cover basic tuning well and these are *Boat Tuning for Speed* by Fred Imhoff and Lex Pranger (Nautical Macmillan, 1975) and *Tuning a Racing Yacht* by Fletcher and Ross (Angus and Robertson, 1972). Both are straightforward, clear and do not get too involved in unnecessary detail.

But small detail does become important at the front of a fleet and that varies from class to class, so what is right for one is often wrong for another. Magazine articles and class newsletters are where the most up to date written information can be found, which may mean turning to foreign magazines for top level tuning tips. The emphasis and quality of a magazine's content depend on editorial policy, so there is no point in giving a complete list of magazines worldwide which cater particularly well for the racing helmsman. Here, though, are a few which are especially strong at present in specialist racing articles: *Regatta* (Germany, all racing), *Yacht Racing and Cruising* (America, strong on good racing articles by top sailors), *Dinghy and Boardsailing* (Britain, deals with small boat and board racing), *Surf* (Germany, boardsailing) and *Seahorse* (Britain, devoted solely to ocean racing).

Back again to books, where some of the secrets of wind and current are well explained by two authors: Ian Proctor in *Sailing Strategy: Wind and Current* (Adlard Coles, 1977) and Alan Watts in *Wind and Sailing Boats* (David and Charles, 1973). Both cover the subject well with Proctor giving all the basic information which every sailor should know and Watts saying more about those vagaries of wind which become more relevant when the basics have been mastered.

Two books together cover the rules as well as any racing helmsman needs them covered. *Elvström Explains the Yacht Racing Rules* gives each rule a brief explanation and provides small plastic boat models so that incidents can be re-played or worked out ashore. My own *The Rules Book* starts from the situation as it occurs on the water and explains the rights-of-way with numbered references to the particular rules which apply. The situations are grouped for easy reference so that right of way rules for starting are in one section with those that apply to a windward leg in the next and so round the course. This simplifies learning the rules and makes post mortem analysis of right of way problems easy. I advise any serious racing helmsman to acquire both books, since together they provide a thorough understanding of the rules. The official IYRU racing rules are printed in both of them.

Sail shape is critical to a boat's motive power and fairly small differences of set make big differences to boat speed. The best basic book on the subject is *Looking at Sails* by Bruce Banks (Nautical Macmillan, 1979) which is straightforward yet manages to go fairly thoroughly into the subject. Almost any club sailor will learn more about his sails and how they work from reading this book. The ultimate work on sails is *Sail Power* by Wallace Ross (Adlard Coles, 1975). It is a book for the more expert and especially for the offshore racer. Much of what a middle-of-the-fleet sailor would learn from this one would be of little use to him.

Knowing how to mount a successful campaign at international level would benefit many and not just potential international sailors either. John Oakeley goes into this in *Winning* (Nautical Publishing Company, 1972, out of print) and in *The Racing Edge* (Channel Press, 1980) Turner and Jobson tell about the preparation and effort involved in a successful America's Cup defence. Above all, the one important message that comes across in both books is: if you're going to attempt to scale the biggest peaks of sailing, get in there and really do the job properly. Otherwise you can forget it – you won't succeed and your efforts would be far better put into something else.

The mental side of sailing has been dealt with previously in only one book, *Go For The Gold* by Garry Hoyt (see page 37). It is a small book, now out of print, which gave more home truths about racing than many twice its size. Written with humour by a sailor who has won much yet doesn't allow losing to affect his enjoyment of the sport, the book (if you can find a used copy) is an excellent one for any sailor who has become over-serious, over-worried about failure and has temporarily forgotten that it is all a wonderful game, something Garry Hoyt reminds us on every page. There are few better books to take to a regatta to remind ourselves of what we are truly capable of doing and to stop us getting paranoid about not being able to do it.

Sometimes a seemingly unrelated book can have great relevance. Such a book is *The Inner Game of Tennis* by Timothy Gallwey (Cape,

1975), which has already begun to affect the competitive approach and attitudes of some of the world's leading sailors. Even so it is not a specialist's book, nor is it primarily a tennis book; it is about human potential and about fulfilling that, whatever your sport.

Although there are many other worthwhile books – it is a mistake to read too many. A few good ones read and then used for reference are far more use than a wall-to-wall nautical library. Stick to four or five good books which are right for your particular sailing standard, written by people who have proved themselves on the water, and you won't become bogged down in details and confused. Combine this reading with regular sailing and racing and the author's words will mean far more than otherwise they would.

In the end experience is the best teacher, but a few well-chosen racing books provide a skipper with an invaluable hot line to the experts, whose advice can be sought on any particular problem.

Observation

Another useful way to research success is to watch races. This is a very underrated way to learn and most people would benefit by making more use of it – not only back markers either. Paul Elvström was surprised just how much he learned in the three years he stopped racing and watched from a power boat: 'I have never learned so much tactics as I learned from that power boat I remember once, it was a big fleet of boats and I went out looking at sails we had made. A friend of mine said "Paul, couldn't you tell me where to go?" I said OK. The next beat I went behind him and said tack and then after a while said tack, then from about number 25 he went up to number three. I think it was very funny because I proved for myself it was right what I did. But that's the only time I did it. It was fun.'

And if someone who has won four gold medals can learn so much from watching sailors less expert than himself, an observant club sailor can learn very much more from watching those who are better than himself. He has a big advantage over those doing more physically difficult sports: he can see everything the expert is doing, if he has a mind to, and can immediately copy it. The expert's tacking technique can never be secret, he cannot conceal the angle of his mast rake; his tiller and sheet movements when sailing down waves cannot be faked; they are all there to be seen, for he is doing them openly. Also by watching, really watching, we enable unconscious learning to happen, learning that bypasses the conscious mind.

Many helmsmen are quite happy to let others learn from them, though some will try to keep their knowledge to themselves. For the middle-of-the-fleet sailor it is usually easy to find someone at the front to tell him anything he needs to know. At higher levels it becomes more difficult. One ex-world champion who had better remain nameless said to a young helmsman who asked about sail settings, 'I had to find it out for myself, I'm damned if I'm going to tell you.' Others say the same but more politely. Though even politeness may not always be what it seems.

At Kiel Week one year Chris Law was checking his mast rake by taking a measurement from the transom to the top of the mast by a tape measure attached to the halyard. Two German Finn sailors saw what was going on and asked if they could see the measurement. Chris was obliging to an extent which was surprising since such measurements are usually considered highly classified information. After the delighted pair had thanked him and gone I expressed my surprise that he should so happily give away any measurement so crucial to boat tune. 'You don't think I'd be that stupid, do you?' Chris replied, 'There's a blank section on the beginning of the tape – the figure they got is 2 inches out.'

In earlier years, though, Chris had asked others exactly the same questions as those two had asked about his boat and mast settings. He had measured champions' boats as they stood unattended in boat parks, he had gone to considerable lengths to find out everything he could about the winner's sails rig and hull. So did Rodney Pattisson in 1967 and early '68 before winning his first gold medal. He talked boats incessantly with other FD sailors and learned from them.

At the 1976 Olympics, Mankin, who had previously won two gold medals, used a strain gauge after it was all over to measure the stress on the spreaders of the Tempest that beat him. In my efforts to find out more than Elvström tells us in his books about how he has done his winning I flew to Denmark to interview him. But for the vast majority of sailors such lengths are quite unnecessary; the go-faster information is far more easily acquired – *provided it is sought.*

When the desired information isn't available on request other methods of finding it out may be necessary. First you must decide exactly what you want to know, which is again why limiting the areas of improvement to be worked on to about three is useful. Only when you know what it is you want to know can you set about finding it out.

When coming to a new class it is always worthwhile asking around the class to find out which manufacturer makes the most successful sails, mast and hull and buy them. Then get someone, the sailmaker perhaps, to show how to set the boat up for different conditions. Once that's done, just sail well and hard, because that's what really makes the difference.

For more detailed study of boat tune, photographs can be useful. One American helmsman moved into FDs from another class and used photography to study details of mast bend and rake. He took photographs from exactly abeam, recording the wind strength at the time of each picture. Once he had the prints he drew a grid of vertical and horizontal lines which enabled him to get exact measurements of mast bend at different positions, spreader height and so on. Then, using the same make of sails and mast, he set up his own boat in exactly the same way, using photos of his own rig in action to check his settings. These ingenious tuning methods combined with regular sailing enabled him to bring his boat tune to a pitch which would otherwise have taken several seasons.

Taking boat tune research to such extremes is certainly going too far, but most don't take their research far enough. And it's not as if it's particularly difficult to do. Coaching courses, reading, watching, getting someone competent to do some coaching or crewing for a winner are all useful ways of finding out those small and big things people do – the way they think, move and act – that enable them to win. For the secrets of sailing success are not so secret and if you really want to know what they all are you can find them out. Some special effort and research may be necessary to uncover them at the top level, but at any other they are no longer secrets and are there for the taking.

9 Reinforcing success

Although eliminating weaknesses in sailing ability is an important part of learning to race more successfully, it is advisable to balance this by making your strong points even stronger. Not only does this make improvement more secure but it ensure that the mind is kept on positive success thoughts, which is important because seeking out mistakes can be demoralizing for some people, who start becoming obsessed by what is wrong.

Building on strengths is therefore an important part of tuning up. Enjoyment is nature's way of enabling you to learn without effort, but some conscious effort can be doubly helpful – not only does it speed up learning but it brings more confidence, a more positive attitude.

There are two ways to reinforce success. The most obvious is by impressing on the rest of the fleet in various ways how good at racing you are, especially after winning. Almost every successful helmsman does so in his own way and small doses of this may help his self-image as a winner and so give him greater confidence to bring out his best in future races. But effort given to psyching out the rest of the fleet is not in the long run very helpful and can rebound. What he is reinforcing is his result, his win, not the abilities and qualities that gave him that result.

The second, and more productive way is to reinforce those abilities and qualities that brought the win. In that way the energies he expends contribute directly to the helmsman's own improvement and are not wasted on changing the attitudes of the rest of the fleet, which is what psyching is mainly about. Whether they see you as better than them, or not, should not be very important, but if you find it is, put your own sailing excellence first and in time their recognition that you have acquired that will follow. Deserve the respect of the rest of the fleet by your abilities and you don't have to demand it by any attempt to psyche them; that respect just comes.

So how can we reinforce our sailing strengths? Well, there are several ways, the most important one being post mortem race analysis. Up to now this has been a way in which the coach-self has been able to recognize mistakes and think through situations so that the same mistake is less likely to recur. Now the technique can be extended to make the good moves – the place-winning ploys, flawless gybes, perfect starts – more likely to recur in future races. What a helmsman does is simply to re-run the successful events in his mind, enjoy them, *feel* himself going through the movements, mentally put himself in the situation.

Daydreaming, that's what it is, though psychologists give it more scientific names. You probably do it anyway, but to most the idea that it is actually doing any good might be surprising, but it does help. Lots of repetitions help even more, since this mental re-playing has been shown in recent research on basketball players to be as effective as physically going through the actions. The daydreaming is to be enjoyed and when the mental repetition of something becomes a chore, stop. It is also a mistake to do repeated mental re-runs of poorly performed actions, for that establishes them more firmly, so be selective about which parts of a race to re-run. Or rather, re-run everything as it should have been done instead of how it was.

This type of mental imagining is something which I have done automatically during my periods of intensive racing. It was a very personal thing and it was therefore something of a surprise to discover that nearly all other keen helmsmen did it too, including Paul Elvström who says, 'You can sail a race in your bed if you like, if you have imagination. I have done that a lot. The more experience you have and the more imagination you have the more likely you are to do the right thing.'

Re-running parts of a race in the mind takes practice, and some people find it easier than others. A written log can be a big help – and not just for those who find mental re-running difficult. Initially, spotting mistakes may not be easy. That doesn't matter. The important thing to begin with is to develop race memory. Once that starts to come post mortem analysis of the race is reasonably easy. And a good race memory is vital. No-one I know who does well is lacking in this department. In my brief but intensive spell in Lasers, I was able to recall the unfolding of every detail of a race and pinpoint not only my own mistakes and good moves but those of everyone I was immediately involved with. Even now, six years later, I can remember a surprising number of situations and parts of those races.

Without a good race memory a sailor who wants to improve is in trouble: he cannot see what is wrong with his races so cannot even begin to put them right. A written log of the events that can be remembered during a race is the best way to develop race memory. And develop it you must for without it you're lost.

A log is valuable in other ways too. It is useful for referring back to much later for some piece of information which may be useful. Before sailing again on a particular stretch of water the log for races held on that same water the previous season can be very helpful. A wind bend which favoured one side of the beat in a westerly last year is almost certain to be there again in the same wind this year. Notes of exactly where the mainsheet traveller was set, what the mainsheet tension was and how the jib fairlead and sheet were adjusted during a particularly successful regatta are all very handy to know three months later when the boat just won't go as fast.

Personally I have never kept a log but would probably have done better if I had. One season it would have been particularly useful. I found that I was lacking a little boat speed, especially when the racing was closest and I really needed that edge of speed. I blamed my boat and sails, naturally. Then I team raced in an event where we sailed other people's boats. In the reputedly fast boat I was given I still didn't have as much speed as I knew I should have, so I began to experiment and found that by easing the mainsheet a few inches the missing speed returned. As I became tense at the height of the competition I was unknowingly pulling in the mainsheet. By letting go a little, all was well. A written log which included a sketch of exactly where the boom end was in relation to the transom during successful races in that wind strength would probably have enabled me to put the problem rights weeks earlier.

A log should include:

Date, location and sketch of the course
Wind strength and direction
Details of current
Note of the bias on the start line
Sails and spars used
A sketch of the route taken round the course
A sketch of the route the winner took (if different)
Position at first mark and finishing position
List of mistakes
Notes about anyone who overtook and reasons why they overtook
Sketches to make it pretty
Funny stories to make you laugh

The number of items and the amount of detail will increase according to the helmsman's skill and time he gives to his racing. Here are some examples of some of the points a national level sailor should be logging:

The honest reason for each and every tack up a bad beat.
Analysis of these reasons will give a good indication of whether he was on top of the racing or the racing was on top of him.
Notes on how the sails and rig were set up, including settings of mast rams, kicking straps and amount of pre-bend in the rig.
A note of wind strength, sea conditions and sail settings during any part of the race when the boat was going extra fast.
Any points noticed about sailing technique, rig, hull or fittings of anyone who went unusually fast – even though they may not have won.
A record of preparation, especially mental, and pre-race warm-up to the race – checking out the wind, practising tacks, and spinnaker work and so on.
Mental attitude before going onto the water, whether it was positive or negative. The feelings about the coming race.
These attitudes before the start.
State of mind during the race and a note of any periods or incidents

in which his state of mind affected sailing, either well or badly.
Any problems with sleep or excessive anxiety during the regatta.
Any intrusion of work, family or financial problems.
Whether girlfriend/wife/boyfriend/husband was present.
Physical condition and the body's ability to do all required of it.
Anything else which might in any way have affected performance.

This is quite a list and only the most dedicated will log everything in such detail, but it is better to record too much than too little. Brief notes are all that are required. Some items will need no coverage while others will require a fair amount.

For those near the front of fleets post mortem analysis of mental attitudes is just as effective as post mortem analysis of tactics. Keith Wilkins discovered this after he had won the European Laser Championship and went the following weekend to a meeting in Wales where about 45 boats were entered. Beforehand he impressed on himself the thought, 'I'm going to win this one.' For the first time he went to a regatta placing a big emphasis on his result, and in conditions which suited him ideally he finished seventh. Recognizing that he prepared himself in the wrong way he has since avoided placing such importance on the result and reverted to paying attention to his technique and sailing skills. It was by doing this that a few weeks later he was able to win the British National Championship with ease. A less perceptive self-coach might have looked to the sail and hull for the explanation for the poor performance, completely missing the real reason.

Reinforcing success mentally can be taken a step further. By imagining his way successfully through crucial parts of a race a helmsman increases his chances of sailing those parts of a race well. In other sports the technique is widely used; it is called mental rehearsal.

There are several criteria for successful mental rehearsal. The important ones are:

It should be done when fairly calm and relaxed.
The rehearsal must be successful (good mark roundings, not bad ones).
More than one rehearsal should be done. Quite how many to do is up to the individual and you'll tend to know when to stop.
It is important to get the feel of the action, not just to be an

observer but to be the doer.

Imagine parts of the race only – for example an ideal start, parts of the first beat, good spinnaker gybes, flawless tacks, overtaking other boats on a reach, gaining places by good tactics on a later beat and so on.

The events should be imagined at the place of competition.

The technique is one I have used inadvertently in daydreaming. I just enjoyed thinking my way past people or imagining myself helping a team mate in a team race, often at odd times like when walking down the street or during boring college lectures. Until recently I hadn't the slightest idea it was doing my sailing any good. That was a surprise, and it was just as surprising to find that other sailors did it too.

Not only does mental rehearsal increase the chances of a good performance, but ability at the practised skills will actually improve them. Winning, remember, starts in the mind. By establishing greater perfection in your mind, you establish a model of the perfect race, which will in time come more nearly to be played out on the water. And although you must always spend a lot of time in and around the boat, you can, with practice, use your mind directly to help improve without being in a boat, except in your imagination. The technique is of most use to more advanced sailors, but it can be helpful for anyone with imagination, and it's an unusually convenient way of practising.

10 Mastering close quarter tactics

There is no better way of mastering boat to boat tactics and rules than by team racing, especially two-a-side team racing. Many will already know at least what team racing is, but for those that don't, it takes place between two teams with an equal number of boats on each side – usually three a side, but sometimes more – and is tactically far more involved than ordinary regatta racing. The helmsmen on one side can win a match not only by sailing faster than their opposition, but they can help each other by deliberately slowing down an opponent to let a team mate overtake and so improve the overall team score.

Close covering, luffing games, tailing boats so they can't tack to lay a weather mark and various techniques using amplified wind shadow can all be used for holding back opposing helmsmen, and all this on top of the full range of tactics and racing skills used in ordinary regatta racing.

The difference between two-boat and most other team racing is that the scoring is altered to take the emphasis even further away from speed round the course, and more towards this tactical infighting. If you were to use the normal ¾ points for first, 2 for second, 3 for third and 4 for fourth scoring, the team which had first boat home would automatically win, provided the other team member infringed no rules. This would obviously be pretty boring. So to liven things up someone had the bright idea of changing the first place points from ¾ to 1¼. This gives many more interesting possibilities. A team which finishes first and fourth now loses to its opponents who finish second and third (5 points beats 5¼). If the team lying first and fourth were to try and win entirely by sailing faster than their opponents, they'd find the odds stacked heavily against them. The man lying fourth would have to overtake and stay ahead of at least one of the two opponents ahead of him, and they wouldn't have to be brilliant tacticians to stop him doing that.

Instead, the losing team can much more easily take the lead by pushing one of their opponents back into last place. The man lying first sacrifices his lead in a close covering battle or luffing match.

So far I've taken for granted that anyone in a team race can, whenever necessary, slow down an opponent and drop him back to last place. Among top level team or match racing helmsmen this would happen with at least the odds of Jimmy Connors winning his service games. But when you first start trying to hold boats back, either by using wind shadow on the beat or by luffing them on reaches they'll often break through.

Two practised helmsmen working together will push an opponent into last place on a beat like this. The leader places himself exactly on the opponent's wind. He then bears away to get really close (quite legal on the beat), but not so close that the other boat must alter course to keep clear. Now he oversheets his mainsail and lets his jib flap, which causes the mainsail to stall, greatly increasing the wind shadow, and slows the boat down. The leeward boat is badly held back since most of her wind supply is cut off.

Usually the leeward boat will be trying to hold her own position by close covering the boat in last place, and during the slowing manoeuvre she continues to do this. That's when the fun really starts. The man in last place tacks to escape and so does the man in the middle of the sandwich in third place, whose tack is covered by the man lying second. The boat trapped in the middle of the sandwich does everything she can to avoid being pushed back to last, most effectively by slowing the last man as she herself is slowed.

The odds are heavily against the boat in the middle of the sandwich if her two opponents know how to work a move which has become known as 'the squeeze'. The man in second place gets as close as he dares to the boat in the middle of the sandwich, then deliberately allows this boat's bow forward until it is about in line with his mast. The boat in the middle of the sandwich is trapped and cannot tack, so the man in last place tacks off in clear wind.

His team mate, who initiated 'the squeeze' now gets his boat moving again to prevent any possibility of the boat he's covering breaking through into a lee bow position. And once the leeward boat is safely back in the centre of wind shadow again the covering boat lets the jib fly, oversheets the mainsail and slows her down. Within half a minute the boat that tacked off will have pulled up from last to second and the 'squeezers', with second and third places, go into the lead.

The manoeuvre takes cool judgement, good boat control and careful timing, but when you can make it work successfully almost every time, you know a lot about wind shadow and covering – enough to be sure of more than holding your own in any ordinary covering duel.

Luffing also becomes a more highly developed art in two-boat team racing. The difference is that it is used as an attacking move rather than as a defensive one; it is used to take an opponent way off course with the sole object of holding him up until a team mate has had time to slip through to leeward. Again, the manoeuvre calls for fine judgement and good timing. The luffing boat must hold the other boat overlapped, easing sheets to slow down and prevent her dipping out of the luff before she's been pushed to back.

The most devastating luffing manoeuvre is reserved for reaching marks. A leading boat lies in wait within the two length circle, stationary. His opponent comes to round the mark and is in a quandary: if he tries to go to leeward of the waiting boat he'll be barging since he has no right to room; if he goes to windward he'll be luffed. He must therefore go to windward and be luffed. In fact there are things he can do to make the luff relatively short lived or even lure the waiting boat outside the two length circle and beat her round the mark. But it doesn't do to give everything away so I'll leave those of you who are intrigued enough by the problem to work it out for yourselves.

There are many other tactical ploys which a losing team can use to pull through into an overall points lead. Many of them are never used in ordinary individual racing, but in all of them there is something to be learned about tactics, rules and boat handling which produces an all-round sharpening up.

Two-boat team racing is also quite a spectator sport. Courses are short and usually laid close to the shore with short legs. The action and place changing give the spectators plenty of excitement, but the stakes mustn't be too high or people start getting over-keen on protesting and the fun goes. Some low-key competitions have been run and it's becoming quite a popular form of competition among some university colleges. For informal competition among friends or the occasional inter-club contest two-boat team racing has a lot to offer. Try it; you'll be surprised what you don't know about covering and close tactics.

For more serious team racing contests three a side is more usual and that too is excellent for learning tactics; it requires more subtle strategy than two a side since there is often the dilemma of whether to go for speed as in an individual race or to slow down and play team tactics. Team racing produces sailors who are tactically very good and experts on the rules, but whose ability to make a boat really move is underdeveloped. British universities do a great deal of team racing whereas the American colleges concentrate on individual sailing, with the result that they produce more sailors of top international standard. Again, it's all a question of balance and some team racing experience is valuable for anyone who has never done any. What's more, its one of the best ways I know of having fun on the water.

11 Good practice makes perfect

In other sports the idea that it is possible to be successful without practising would be thought ridiculous. For keen golfers, cricketers, tennis players, gymnasts, runners and the rest, practising is part of their way of life. Even mediocre levels of performance in those sports cannot be attained without it. Yet the vast majority of competitive sailors don't regard practice as necessary, even though they might claim they want to improve and would enjoy finishing higher in their races.

Sailors have been unusually slow to realize that what is true for other sports is also true for theirs: that practising not only works but is by far the most effective single method of giving an all-round boost to racing performance. Elvström, Pattisson, Bertrand, to name but three, were giving more time to practising than any of their opposition at the times they dominated the world in their chosen classes. Keith Wilkins used solo practice, some reading but no racing, to raise his standard in five months to a level which would otherwise have taken at least two years.

In any sailor's quest for success, whether a beginner or expert, his greatest ally is good practice. The emphasis, though, is on *good*. And good practice means working on particular skills and techniques; it also means regular practice – at least once a week. The beauty of solo practice is that you can work on a wide range of techniques and abilities without having to rely on anyone else except your crew and perhaps some emergency rescue service being present. The list of items solo practice can help with includes:

Tacking
Gybing
Heavy weather techniques
Keeping a dinghy level
Windshift spotting
Starting
Mark rounding
Wave technique
Spinnaker hoists, drops and gybes
Physical fitness
Helmsman and crew co-ordination
Self-confidence
Sailing speed and the intuitive 'feel' side of sailing.

Quite a list. So what is good practice for each of these items? To be good, the practice must be planned, not aimless. That means having in mind what is to be worked on and making a practice plan to include those items. The best way to go about that is to write down beforehand what is to be practised and how it's to be practised, for the clearer idea a sailor has of what he wants to gain from the practice the more likely he is to gain it. The list should not be long, since more is gained by practising a few things well than many poorly. It should also be varied from session to session so the practice never drops to the level of dull routine.

Good practice is also patient practice in which one thing at a time is worked on, though without overpractising by spending too long on any one item. The aim is long term improvement so it is neither necessary nor desirable to hammer away at one skill to try and perfect that in one afternoon. Instead a few items should be worked on for just long enough to make some improvement, however small, and then move on to the next. The idea is not to strive and fight too hard to acquire a skill but rather to absorb skills so that they become part of you. Nor should you mentally beat yourself with a stick when you fail to get something right. Learning is primarily a subconscious process and if you try to *make* yourself learn instead of *allowing* the learning to happen, you block the unconscious learning by mental striving.

Experiment, too, is part of good practising, deliberately trying different ways of doing things. Only in that way can you be sure you have found the best. But above all don't expect quick results from practice sessions. Some improvement may certainly come from one period of practice, but far greater and more permanent change comes from a dozen. And that is what you should be looking for.

For anyone it will mean racing less, sailing more and doing more homework. Someone in, say, their third season can make considerable progress by giving two hours a week to their sailing – one hour on the water and one hour ashore. Their time afloat can also be used better by missing some races in order either to do solo practice or to watch. Solo practice while others are racing may not be so much fun and feel anti-social, in which case it should be done at other times, but watching the occasional race – even if that does seem strange – should be done, especially by a helmsman who has been stuck at a similar level for a season or two. Improving means breaking old habits and breaking the habit of racing every time he goes to the club is a good start, quite apart from what can be learned.

The whole method is a way of directing all your mental and physical efforts in the most productive way. Those who can do this anyway are the ones who already win races. They have little else in common, being drawn from the ranks of the clever, the fairly thick, the big, the small, the impoverished, the wealthy, the bullshitters and even the meek – it doesn't seem to matter. And anyone else who previously didn't apply themselves in the most productive way now can. If they want to.

The method of putting together a self-coaching plan is exactly the same, whatever a helmsman's standard or class of boat. After a few weeks or months it is necessary to review the weakest areas. One problem area will probably be resolved quickly while a new one emerges as needing attention. And so it goes on. While it is a good idea to make a self-coaching timetable to keep on the right track, the self-coaching techniques are there to serve you in the perfection of the art, not as exercises you become slaves to.

To some all this might seem an over-systematic and even joyless way to get better at sailing. Few will doubt that it works but, it could be said, so does getting fit by running a mile a day through a swamp in hobnailed boots carrying sandbags. But nothing I have suggested is in the least unenjoyable. All that might be unenjoyable is *the thought* of breaking old habits. But only the thought. Once the self-coaching has begun, as those who have tried it confirm, the benefits and improvement bring their own rewards and racing becomes more enjoyable, not less.

Tacking

Go out and begin by doing lots of tacks, as a warm-up and for the exercise before going into more detailed practice. Next sail close-hauled for a few lengths, then put in a tack about every ten seconds (longer for larger boats). After ten tacks stop and rest. Do the same again but this time deliberately vary the speed. Dinghy sailors should do a series of tacks which are over-rolled, followed by another series under-rolled. This practice should not go on for too long, usually no more than ten minutes, and should end with a sequence of tacks which are as well executed as you can manage. By working regularly in this way you will find the most efficient tacks for any wind strength. Deliberately varying the method during practice means that a particularly good tacking technique will emerge, almost on its own.

It is important to leaf your way through the tacks, being aware of all the movements you are making and occasionally stopping to think your way through a tack (this is especially important for the crew) to discover whether there are any unnecessary or clumsy moves. Non-trapeze crews in dinghies which have thwarts, for example, often sit in the boat on the thwart before getting their bottoms out over the side. Two moves instead of one, which makes the tack slower and deprives the helmsman of that all-important bite of righting moment immediately after the tack which would enable him to get the boat immediately into top gear again. The crew should also think about which way he is facing during the tack. Sometimes a boat's tacking is transformed when the crew reverses the way he faces during a tack. Again it's a matter of trial and error.

In the work-up to their successful America's Cup defence, Turner and Jobson regularly used to put *Courageous* through sequences of 50 consecutive tacks. Match races are often decided on tacking ability so on *Courageous* they worked extra hard to reach the highest standard of tacking. But good tacking is vital in any racing and the highest standard is there for anyone to reach who decides to do so.

Gybing

Gybing a non-spinnaker boat will be dealt with first; spinnaker gybing comes later. Repetition is again the key to practice. In lightish winds it is best to do repeated roll-gybes, pausing to rest and assess whether the gybes can be improved – or just pausing to rest.

In heavy weather the fun starts, and it is better to begin by gybing in the lulls so the session does not just become boat righting practice. Once gybing in the lulls feels easy, re-introduce excitement by gybing in the moderate gusts and graduate, if all is going well, to gybes in the biggest gusts of the day. In these it might well be a feat of heroic proportions even to attempt a gybe, let alone come out the other side upright, but try it anyway. In less extreme wind the best practice is to throw a string of gybes one after the other until they become easy.

I discovered the benefits of gybing practice by accident. Just after I had started sailing the Laser, I was due to write an article for a yachting magazine and, as sometimes happens, was a bit stuck for something to write about, so decided to do a piece on gybing. To see just how I did my gybes, more as research for the article than anything else, I went out and did a series of gybes and studied my technique. I saw things that weren't quite right so, in the lighter spells, did repeated gybes to iron out the flaws. Then I became bolder and started gybing in the heavier stuff, until finally the hardest gusts of the day no longer presented any problems, whereas an hour earlier they probably would have done.

The improvement in gybing technique itself was valuable enough but, as I discovered in the next few heavy weather races, there was another benefit. The usual anxiety about gybing had gone, which was quite liberating. Although the experience of going down a first reach terrified out of your mind may have a certain perverse fascination, it's much more fun if you're so confident about the gybe to come that you're almost looking forward to it. And once the fear of gybing in a force six has been conquered, so has heavy weather fear– a condition from which many more helmsmen and crews suffer than would ever admit.

There are some forms of practice which conveniently combine tacking and gybing. One is to do what in America they call spinners, where the boat is spun round, tacking and gybing through a whole series of 720° turns until helmsman and crew are almost dizzy, at which point they break off and spin in the opposite direction. The best combined practice is to sail a slalom course, beating up through a line of closely spaced buoys and then gybing back through them on a run. In a steady wind you can compete against yourself by timing the runs and trying to beat your own best time.

Heavy weather

Far and away your best heavy weather teacher is enjoyment. So when it's blowing get out there and have a ball. Reef if necessary, or even go out with jib only if it's really hairy, and play. It doesn't matter much what you do – reach up and down, try some beating if you feel like it – just so long as you have fun. Enjoyment is the most undemanding of teachers, too; she demands no theory, no studiously written work programme nor any other obvious mental effort. You don't even know she's teaching you. All you know is that by keeping her company on windy days mastery of the boat and the elements just comes. Without knowing quite how it happened, you start to become good in a blow.

Then of course you want to become still better in a blow. And we have no choice but to bring the old mind to bear on the problem again. But don't for goodness sake let it elbow enjoyment aside: whatever you're wanting to improve or learn, never turn your back on her – she's your greatest ally.

But let's keep intellect out of heavy weather a little longer yet. Sail without the rudder. Yes, take it off and get out there. That is of course if you sail a dinghy and it has a pivoting plate rather than a dagger board; with any other kind of boat it won't work (boards apart). The beauty of this kind of heavy weather practice is that to begin with you don't have to do it in heavy weather – force three will do very nicely.

Applying the rudder, anyway, is the worst way to steer a dinghy on smooth water; if you want to helm the boat most efficiently, that is. As every sailing book you ever pick up is quick to point out, the rudder acts as a brake every time you angle it to alter course, which is why the boat is best controlled with absolute minimum of rudder movements. The other two methods of controlling the boat's direction don't slow her down: heeling and sail trim. A windward heel bears her away, a leeward heel heads her up. Playing the sheets provides more immediate and sensitive control over the boat's direction than heeling. Ease the jib and sheet in the main to head up, sheet in the jib and ease the main to bear away. Combine angle of heel with sheet adjustments and you can make the boat do just whatever you like.

When you want to tack . . . get out there and do it. When you can make a boat do what you want it to do in a force three without a rudder you'll get the most out of the boat in a force six with rudder. Anyone who spends his time in heavy weather fighting the helm is relying too much on his rudder and too little on boat trim and sail sheeting. Get these last two right and the rudder becomes what it should be – a fine adjustment control for making frequent but tiny alterations of course. But don't forget to lift the plate half up and don't try it in a boat with a dagger board.

That leaves gusts. Mastery of these comes automatically by regular practice of windward heeling and upright sailing and by sailing without a rudder. If it isn't coming it's most likely because you're not looking upwind often enough to see what's coming. Once you can read the water accurately for gusts, heavy weather life becomes much easier. One other tip: at the back end of the gust when you're beating, don't bear off, pinch up.

Keeping a dinghy level

As I've been on about upright sailing in dinghies enough already I shall say no more, except that it really is all-important in heavy weather and the ways suggested to develop it in Chapter 4 work excellently. Keel-boat sailors should think in terms of an optimum angle of heel, the angle at which they make their maximum windward speed and beyond which the boat makes excess leeway and slows down, so when they read the word 'upright' they should substitute 'optimum angle of heel'.

Windshift spotting

As in the section on pages 50–54.

Starting

As in the section on pages 45–50.

Mark rounding

Smooth, fast mark rounding is most important on estuaries and inland water, but even on big sea courses, marks provide opportunities for gaining places, so good mark rounding always pays – a bad rounding puts you a step or two down that moving escalator.

It is best to start the practice on the easiest of rounding, a reach to a beat. Aim to start the turn wide so as to be close hauled on passing the mark, being sure to leave only a few inches of water between it and the side of the boat. Go closer than would ever be sensible in a race. Faults to look out for are: allowing the boat to heel if it is a dinghy; the crew pulling the jib in too fast; the helmsman not pulling the mainsail in fast enough. It is worth paying a great deal of attention to detail during each practice session until all these points are as near perfect as can be.

Turning from a run to a beat is much more difficult, so it is better not even to attempt it until the other rounding is nearly perfect. All the same points apply, though here the line of the turn is more difficult to get right and requires special attention during practice. If the repetitions are inclined to be boring, mark each one out of ten; it keeps the interest up. After a few weeks of this when immaculate roundings have become the norm, include a gybe in the rounding.

When all that happens flawlessly, time and time again, the real enthusiast can take the game an intriguing step further. He can take his rudder off and perfect rudderless mark rounding (provided his boat is one that will allow that). In doing so he will learn much, much more than close to the buoy skills; he will gain complete mastery of boat handling.

But, some will ask, is all this really necessary just to gain the odd half length at a mark? It all depends how much that half length means to you. If you are a perfectionist anything wrongly done is not good enough, and by perfecting one ability others benefit. The practice also contributes to race concentration and, because of the benefit inherent in it, is enjoyable. If that benefit is not felt, no, it is not worthwhile. Certainly I have always felt the benefit of mark rounding practice and have often done it outside races as do most sailing champions. This isn't just true of sailing giants either. The great cellist Pablo Casals was discovered by one of his pupils practising bowing long single notes on an open string – the very exercise a child first learns.

'You of all people,' she exclaimed, 'surely you don't need to do that!'

'When you have truly mastered this,' Casals replied, 'you have mastered the instrument.'

Exactly the same is true of the most basic sailing skills.

Wave technique

Go out on a day when there are waves and just sail among them with enjoyment as your teacher. They are alive; make the boat come to life among them. Experiment, throw your weight about to propel the boat on a surfing plane. Work the sheets and tiller to give all the speed that's going down the waves, trying always to keep the hull sailing downhill and avoiding stonewalling into the wave ahead. Whenever a power boat passes use its wake to get you up onto the plane. Upwind the smooth movement of the hull through the water matters more than anything, so go for that, even if it means weaving several feet off course to miss a big crest. Again, experiment – see what is possible and what is not, what stops the boat and what makes it take off. Every time there are waves go out and play among them. Know the theory of wave sailing too, but of the sailing abilities this is the one which in the end is all feel, and no books are going to teach you that. Your teacher is enjoyment, the sheer joy of getting out there in a force five in the sunshine and doing it.

Spinnaker hoists, drops and gybes

Solo practice is the only way to develop flawless and very fast spinnaker work. The secret behind doing that is not to go for speed. Start slowly. Make each move smoothly and deliberately, if necessary stopping to repeat a step several times until the best moves are found. Work in this way for several weeks and speed will come. Most spinnaker foul-ups happen because someone gets a move wrong or gets the moves right, but in the wrong order. Either of these happen because the moves themselves are not secure enough so that rushing them causes a breakdown in the sequence.

Get the moves right and the sequence secure, then there will be no need to rush; it will just happen fast and with far fewer mishaps.

After the basics have been worked up in this way, and only then, many repetitions should be introduced into the practice – say ten hoists and drops in a row, then ten spinnaker gybes. But whenever there is a foul-up stop, work out why and go back to slower, methodical practice in which you get to know and feel every move. Practice in which everything is done right is by far the best kind, even if the hoists and gybes are all slow. After a few weeks they won't be: they'll be faster and less accident prone than anyone else's.

Don't expect the benefits gained in practice to be immediately transferable to races. They may be, but then again they may not. When working with Scottish youngsters on a coaching course I made some of them practise their spinnaker work slowly and systematically and before long they were hoisting, lowering and gybing their spinnakers quite smoothly without snarl-ups. Already, some of them were doing their spinnaker work faster when doing this slow practice than when trying to do it fast during the race, and that was after only half an hour of practice.

In the race that followed some of them were out to show just how fast they could now do their hoists, but the spinnaker work in nearly every boat ended up slower than when practising with the emphasis only on doing everything right, not on speed. As far as spinnaker work goes (and many other skills too) we can add a corollary to the old saying 'more haste less speed'. It is, 'more perfection more speed'. And that perfection comes from regular practice in which the emphasis is on getting every move right, however much it may be necessary to slow the procedure down to achieve that.

For real perfectionists here's something to introduce into the practice to make it more difficult. (That, as we saw earlier, is an excellent way of making a skill totally secure during the pressures of a race.) The method is to blindfold the crew. He then has to rely on feeling his way about the boat, on experiencing every movement fully and not be distracted by what he is seeing. This anchors him in the present moment and stops him doing one job while his mind in rushing on to the next. Even the most experienced crews can learn a good deal from doing this.

Offshore crews might also benefit from this kind of practice, as experience with blind sailors has shown. At a sailing course for the blind a few years ago held in 35-foot cruiser racers the crews were made to do spinnaker hoists and drops, just as any sighted crew would. To begin with they were slow and hesitant as they felt their way into the job, but after a few days the sail was going up and down very satisfactorily. Towards the end of the week they set off on an overnight cruise and were sailing at dusk with the spinnaker set. The sighted skipper said that in the interests of good seamanship they should drop the spinnaker as it would soon be dark. 'What difference does that make?' asked one of them, to the skipper's acute embarrassment. This sightless crew, most of whom had not sailed before, were better at night time sail-handling than almost any offshore crew for they had been practising in the dark all week.

Physical fitness

Sailing two or three times a week automatically brings a certain amount of physical fitness and the harder you push yourself the fitter you're going to get. At club level this may well be enough, but not at regional or national level.

Helmsman and crew co-ordination

Solo practice automatically improves helmsman and crew teamwork, provided they work on specific abilities in a careful and perfectionist way. On offshore yachts practice is particularly helpful. Everyone's tasks can be clearly delegated and practised so that every drill works like clockwork. Video can be useful for having a look at all the moves later and working out any better ways in which things can be done.

Self-confidence

By working in the right way we gain useful spin off – benefits which we didn't consciously work for and didn't expect. With solo practice self-confidence is one of these; we get a good psychological boost which, because it is built on the secure foundation of improved technique rather than the quicksands of ego psyching, won't crumble because of one bad race or the psyching out efforts of others.

Sailing speed and the intuitive 'feel' side of sailing

For those who are less expert, sailing speed is something which improves automatically through good solo practice; it can help the front-runners too. By spending time in the boat a helmsman gains greater control and more 'feel' for the boat. This 'feel' for sailing, which all the true natural sailors have, seems to be directly related in some way to boat speed. They may make mistakes, but real 'seat of the pants' sailors who have that natural feel for sailing invariably go fast – even in the wrong directions. So if we acquire more of that 'feel' we will go faster. Keith Wilkins has found that and so has Buddy Melges, gold medallist in the Solings at Kiel. Why it's true I don't know, but true it is.

To begin with in solo practice it is important to get the basic sailing skills right: upright sailing, beating with the luff of the jib just on the point of lifting, mainsheet and traveller set so the luff of the mainsail lifts at exactly the same time as the jib or marginally before. Once all that starts to become second nature you can set about consciously developing more 'feel'.

Feel is a combination of bodily sensation, balance and hearing. More may well be involved. The more you expand your awareness through these senses the more 'feel' you have. It is this expanded awareness that the natural sailor has. When this is experienced your sense of identity begins to merge with the boat. A sailor whose senses are dull can sail his boat into a floating plank of wood without flinching, but the sailor whose sailing awareness has so expanded that he becomes one with the boat will not only flinch as his boat hits the wood, the impact will almost hurt him – even though it is seemingly no more than an impact between two inanimate objects. For the true sailor, though, the boat is not inanimate: he brings it to life because it becomes part of him. And if you are to become a true sailor that is what you must do. Then, for example, you don't need to read books to tell you how to handle waves, you feel when you've got it right and the boat screams at you when you get it wrong. Then automatically you make every movement of tiller and mainsheet to produce the greatest speed the hull is capable of through, over or round the waves.

Instead now of directing your main awareness towards what you see, bring it to what you feel: the pull on the tiller arm, the tension in your sitting out muscles, the pressure between your buttocks and the side of the boat, the wind on your face and head, the wetness of the spray. You cannot do all of these at once, so do them one at a time. While doing so, just sail the boat. Sail it well and also sail it badly, deliberately, getting the feeling of what happens when you point too high or sail too low on the beat. The renowned Finn sailor Henry Sprague used to sail at night lying on the deck to experience more fully this feeling side of sailing. Edward Warden-Owen, winner of several British national championships, used to practise blindfold and claims to have gained may 'unseen' benefits from that.

When you begin to turn your attention inwards on yourself, on your feelings and sensations, sailing becomes a meditation. You are not racing; you are entering fully into the experience of sailing, becoming one with the boat. You begin to live in the present, not thinking about the past or the future, just enjoying the sensations of sailing a boat, entering into those sensations in a way that your striving never allows you to do in a race. Thoughts may wander to other things and when they do bring them gently back to the boat, to the sound of the bow wave, the sight of the hull moving through the water, whatever most strongly draws your attention.

It was Melges who said: 'I love to completely involve my mind, my body and all my sense with the boat and her path in the water. I believe it is this concentration that allows us to sail without competition as much as we do, yet have speed equal to all. I very seldom watch the sails. Rather, a blank stare at the horizon forward gives me the angle of attack.' Notice that he refers to that absorption as concentration. Notice too that in this state of expanded awareness the sense of sight becomes far less important. None of that visual policing of the jib luff to stop it catching you out and luffing; instead a 'blank stare at the horizon'.

Although Melges experiences this oneness with his boat and the elements, the wind and water, more intensely than most and expresses it more articulately, every successful sailor experiences some heightening of the senses and perception when he is sailing at his best. In that state mistakes just don't seem to happen; everything is right and winning seems a natural and inevitable result of that.

Most successful sailors associate that state, or their own version of it, with their best performance, something that comes as a result of sailing really well. Which is true, but only half of the truth. The other half is that you can acquire that state itself and as a result of acquiring that, your best abilities will be available to you. That is a new tack for most people to take, but it is a very fruitful one, and one which begins with solo sailing, as many of the world's most successful sailors have discovered.

So far here, and in my previous books, I have been very analytical about all the various techniques and tactics of sailing. Yet that is only a stage on the journey, a necessary stage, which can later be left behind – not forgotten, but not thought too much about either. Tactics then become more spontaneous and intuitive, as they are for Melges: 'I have no "rule of thumb" concerning tactics. They are all done on impression when in the open sea. This feel cannot be explained, but I find it is right more times than it is wrong.'

When we leave the intricacies of detail behind and just sail for all we're worth, our sailing, like a concert pianist's playing, becomes inspired and we're worth more than we realized. Then we excel ourselves and fulfil more of the potential that is truly ours to fulfil.

12 Paired practice

Solo practice will give only so much; practising in pairs will give almost all the rest, enabling you to work up any racing ability except big fleet tactics or the special mental qualities needed to cope with the pressures of big events. Pairing up with someone else is usually spontaneous: two brothers having fun races together or helmsmen of similar standard who are friends going out between races for some practice. But working with someone of similar standard who you get on well with can be so helpful that it's worth setting out to find a sparring partner.

There are many advantages of working in this way. In the first place it's more sociable than working on your own and two people tend to keep each other going – less self-discipline is needed than with an entirely solo effort. Essential as solo practice is, it cannot develop boat tune or tactics in the way that paired practice can. Nor does it introduce the competitive element, which paired practice does.

Before and after races, too, it is very helpful to have someone to work with. Some pre-race planning can be done together before the start: such things as the right end of the start line, the best way up the first beat, any tidal effects, can all be thought out together. After the race it is very handy to have a colleague who was in the thick of it with you so that you can analyse why one side of the beat was favourable and the other wasn't, what went wrong after the start when things were looking good, why you were going slowly on the reaches, and so on.

There will often be people in your club with whom you can have this kind of conversation at the bar after races anyway, but the analysis gets you much further in finding out where you went wrong and how you can put that right for the next time if the person you're talking to is your training partner. Not only do you have his expert advice and observations on what you could do to improve, but you also learn by working out why he went wrong and how he might do things differently next time. Two lessons for the price of one.

This pairing up with someone else is such an obvious idea that most people haven't thought of it. If it doesn't happen by chance, the chances are it doesn't happen – most people don't go out of their way to make it happen. But when two people do get together the results are often spectacular.

In my own case it happened by chance. My brother is a year younger than me and when we were in our mid teens we spent much of our summer holidays fooling around in boats. The boats happened to be one design so we naturally spent a lot of time sailing races to every corner of the lake. After two summers of this we were both finishing at the front of the club fleet.

Four times British 470 national champion and Kiel Week winner Eddie Warden-Owen benefited even more startlingly from informal training with his brother. He was 20 in the year that they practised intensively together, going out many evenings a week and sometimes during the day, sailing short courses round mooring buoys, practising tacking every five seconds, competing to see who could raise and lower the spinnaker fastest and generally sharpening up most things that matter. Before that summer's practice Eddie had been a moderately good club sailor, but no more than that. Afterwards he had the ability and technique to win open meetings and the following year won his first national championship in the highly competitive GP14 class. His brother too went on to become GP national champion.

To practise most effectively in pairs it is important, as it is with solo practice, to decide what you're going to practise. The best way is to write down a brief list of items to be worked on. Then decide exactly how to practise each of the items.

There are seven kinds of paired practice, which are described below, and each works on very different skills and abilities, so it is most important to pick the kind of paired practice that is going to improve the thing you want to improve, not something else. Two Icelandic sailors, for example, trained all winter together but failed to develop their best boat speed or learn windshift tactics because all they were trying to do was beat each other.

Match racing

The two boats race around a normal course, preferably a shortish course. They can start by the gate start method where one sails on port and the other starts by crossing close under her stern. All that matters is winning, so as soon as one gets ahead he should close cover. Match racing is only of limited value and should not be practised too much for the same reason any racing holds back improvement if over-indulged: bad habits solidify and perfection is never achieved. But done in moderation match racing is excellent for boat handling and covering practice and, to some extent, rules. It is not much use, as the Icelanders discovered, for boat speed, windshift tactics, starting or tuning. For those we need other methods.

Clear wind paired practice

Here we make it a strict rule that neither helmsman may sit on the other's wind. The start and course are the same as before but now the race is decided by making the boat go fast and reading the windshifts rather than covering ability. As these are the two most important race-winning abilities of all, this type of paired practice is extremely valuable.

Speed sailing

This time interest is entirely in the relative speed of the boats through the water. Both sail on the same tacks, and very long ones too, a few lengths apart, again keeping each others' wind clear. There is no need to sail a course, only to sail as fast as possible in clear wind close together to see who can go faster on one long tack. Sailing speed then becomes the only variable, so a lift which one helmsman fails to respond to immediately, differences in boat tune, poor wave handling by one helmsman or anything else that affects speed will show up. If one boat goes consistently faster, the helmsmen swap boats and so establish whether it is the boat or the helmsman that is slow. If it is the helmsman he can learn from his friend what he's doing wrong. If the boat is at fault it can be set up exactly like the other, and that will even them up.

Downwind practice is often neglected but shouldn't be because it is extremely valuable for developing that extra turn of reaching speed which wins so many major races these days.

Boat handling

Here we are interested in efficient tacking, gybing and spinnaker handling. All these are better worked up first by several weeks of solo practice and then put to the test by paired practice. The way to test tacking ability is to sail a short beat keeping in clear wind and putting in a tack every five seconds. Gybing is tested on the run in the same way. Spinnaker work can't be made quite so obviously competitive, but hoisting and dropping at the blast of a whistle will show up which is handling their chute more efficiently.

You can also watch each other's efforts and criticize the other's faults or copy some tricks and shortcuts which they've worked out that you hadn't thought of.

For many people solo practice is the best way of perfecting these skills, especially working in the way suggested in the last chapter. Others need the spur of real live competition to push them to faster and more efficient spinnaker work, tacks and gybes and for these competitors paired practice is the answer.

Starting

This has already been described on pages 45–50.

Special practice

Rudderless races in pairs are excellent for improving boat handling and control. Races in which the helmsmen are blindfolded are also unusually good practice.

Discovering local knowledge

To discover the wind and tide patterns of a particular piece of sailing water, the two boats start together and take opposite sides of the beat to see who gets to the weather mark ahead. Provided the two are of about equal speed this shows which side of the course is favoured and is very useful practice over a championship sailing area in the days before the event begins.

To make the best use of paired practice it is important to understand these different types of practice and the benefits of each. Then it is possible to select the right kinds of practice to work on the particular problem areas of the moment. To begin with it will be necessary to write down the exact form a practice session will take, but in time that will not be necessary. A log is also useful as notes about how a previous practice went can help in planning a future one. For all but the real experts the ideal form of practice is to combine solo and paired practice: an hour of solo practice first and then an hour or more working together. But for someone right at the top of a class of great complexity like the FD working with someone of similar ability is the best way.

Rodney Pattisson is so convinced of the benefits of practising in pairs that he hardly practises any other way. He and his sparring partner take to the water for up to seven hours a day during the months before the Olympics. The working programme is far more intense than most people could handle, since Pattisson believes in working, working and then, after a rest is long overdue, carrying on working. At times only darkness curtails his practice. His method is mainly to do speed sailing in a systematic and very basic way. He and his aparring partner go out in two FDs accompanied usually by a support boat laden with sails. The two FDs race together for hours, stopping from time to time to swap sails or make adjustments to jib sheeting positions, mast rake or anything else that might usefully be changed. During the racing small adjustments to the mainsail luff tension, foot tension or kicker happen as a matter of course, though one boat might sometimes sail with these fixed while the other helmsman makes adjustments in order to identify the optimum setting for that wind strength.

The changes are always carefully selected and only one thing at a time is changed. The effect of that change is then assessed by sailing together, and in this way Pattisson builds up an enormous store of knowledge on the optimum settings of all the adjustments he can make while sailing and best sails for any particular wind strength. In his work-up to his first gold medal in 1968 he had all the settings calibrated and written down in a notebook. Since then he has tended to be less rigorous in his recording methods, relying more on an unusually good memory. Neither would the swaps be confined to sails; he and his crew often swap boats with his sparring partners and it's not unknown for him to switch masts while pitching around in a force four several miles offshore.

While this fine boat tuning proceeds another equally important thing is happening – Pattisson's and his crew's own sailing skills are being developed to the highest level. He contends that this is the only real way to practise, and he doesn't need to argue the point – all his world championship wins, two gold medals and a silver do that.

There is a good deal of evidence to show that paired practice alone is more effective than the kind of group training that is part of many countries' Olympic work-up. Since 1968 Pattisson has excused himself from the organized Olympic squad training and used this paired training system. In 1976 when Britain was becoming internationally strong in the 470 class for the first time the places in the national training squad were limited to eight. Two who were denied entry to the squad, Jim Saltenstall and Nigel Barrow, got together and put in a lot of practice together. After three months they were given permission to join the squad's practice races, though they still couldn't train with the squad. To everyone's surprise they were now the fastest 470s on the water, tending to finish first and second in the practice races. Nigel Barrow went on to take second place in the trials – a handsome improvement from being ranked ninth, and beating people who had the supposed advantage of partaking in the group training.

Although these are near professionals, a similar approach can be applied at all levels. It is simply that working with one other boat is a very efficient way to improve your racing standard, especially if the sailor you're working with has a sharp mind, parallel sailing ambitions and is of about your own standard. For most of us there is neither the necessary ambition, time nor inclination to take things as far as the Olympic aspirants, but excellent results can be gained by employing the same basic approach at club level, giving over only two or three hours a week to practising.

The working relationship that develops can help in many different ways. No two helmsmen have the same strengths and weaknesses, even when they are of the same standard. One might do best in heavy weather, the other in light air; one may be an ace on the starting line, the other a lone wolf who knows how to make a boat go super fast; one might be a rules buff, the other really clued up on sail shapes. The great thing about two people sharing all their racing secrets is that they both help each other to improve their weaker areas.

If you are consistently being thrashed in light air by your sparring partner, he'll tell you why; if you leave him behind in a blow, you'll tell him what he's doing wrong. So you become each other's coaches. And just to have someone to really talk things through with is a great help. Often in the course of talking a problem through you find the answers yourself, but you're less likely to find those answers if you don't talk the problem through with anybody.

In this way your racing thinking becomes more focused. You no longer stand still and you can break out of a doldrum period where you just don't seem to be getting any better. Races are sailed and enjoyed as usual, but afterwards you can discuss the lessons that come out of the race and once you've worked out what you did wrong, you can plan how to practise and work at these weak areas so the mistakes don't recur.

13 Physical fitness

Many are the reasons why sailors turn to fitness training, not all of them entirely praiseworthy:

> 'The others do it so I'd better.'
> 'The others aren't doing it so I will.'
> 'It must be good for you, it hurts.'
> 'It will make me feel sharper and clearer-headed.'
> 'It will stop me getting worn out and inefficient in heavy weather.'

The reasons get better towards the bottom of the list, with the last two the only valid ones. The benefits from training are greatest in heavy weather races when a fit body is better able to cope with the demands made on it, which leaves the mind free to make good decisions, however tough the going gets. But in all conditions an all-round feeling of well-being often arises from regular fitness training. Frequent sailing provides the same physical glow but not everyone sails often enough to give themselves that, so some other kinds of exercising may be needed. Besides, that fine healthy, alert feeling that comes from being in good physical shape is worth having, whether it's of immediate benefit to racing or not.

Levels of physical fitness beyond that basic one, which can be acquired by regular exercise, should always be according to need. And those who don't have that basic level need to acquire it, for without it even medium weather races can over-extend a very unfit body, causing exhaustion, loss of concentration and mistakes. It is also worth remembering that everyone over the age of 25 grossly underestimates their physical fitness, yet becoming fit need not be a field day for masochists. Nor should it be, so read on.

Anyone whose immediate goal is national or international level racing must physically be very fit. In strong winds this can, and often does, make all the difference; in lighter winds too physical fitness, though not of the stamina and strength variety, does play a beneficial part. Physical fitness is more than being able to sit out longer and harder than anyone else, though that is important; it includes an all-round toning up of the body so that it as well equipped as possible to do everything required of it during a race. Such faculties as balance, bodily awareness and the ability to move cat-like about a boat are all physical: they all contribute to sailing ability – a helmsman lacking them is clumsy and has no feel for his boat and developing those physical abilities must be part of any complete, all-round physical training programme.

There are several ways in which we can work up physical fitness. These are:

Sailing
Running
Gymnastic exercises
Dancing
Yoga
Other sports
Diet

There is variety enough here to suit everyone's needs, so let's look at each activity in turn and see what each will and will not provide for us.

Sailing

Daily sailing in a dinghy or sailboard is quite fit-making provided the winds are moderate or strong. The big advantage of using sailing to get oneself fit for sailing is that it tones up and strengthens all the muscles required in a race; it also develops bodily awareness, especially if the sailor takes his attention from time to time to the sensations of his body during practice and becomes more conscious of movement and physical sensations.

Some manoeuvres make sailing more physically demanding than normal, so provide good fitness training. These include series of tacks, say twenty in a row, with no more than a couple of boat lengths' sailing between each, then another twenty and so on until exhausted. Then do another twenty. Righting a capsize is also very good exercise in a single-hander so when using part of a practice session primarily as fitness training the boat should be deliberately capsized when you are already fairly exhausted. That is good for stamina and simulates what may happen in a race, which means a capsize late in a race will be less disastrous when next it occurs.

Another good form of stamina training is to sail beats which are longer than you will ever come across in a race – say one and a half times or twice as long – so that the body becomes accustomed to long, gruelling beats which are more demanding than in a race. This makes a tough championship beat more manageable and gives you something to spare over those who only sail normal-length beats. Do not, though, make sitting out tougher by wearing excessive weight. Ordinary weight jackets do damage to the body, especially knee cartilages and backs, so it would be silly to court injury further by overloading already highly stressed parts of the body.

Sailing other livelier classes is a good way to become fitter. Laser sailors who moved to Finns have shown themselves physically superior, especially in mobility but also in stamina, than long-term Finn sailors. The best possible fitness training for trapeze crews is boardsailing, though without a harness. Not only does this exercise all the muscles a trapezing crew uses but it opens up much greater bodily awareness and feel for the wind and waves than crewing can ever do.

One way to beef up arm and shoulder muscles is to take the mainsheet direct from the centre of the boom on reaches to give a one-to-one pull. Then pump down the waves. You are practising, remember, so anything goes. In the race stick by the rules, but if you want to one-purchase the mainsheet on a Laser (which the class rules forbid) or pump a lot (which the IYRU forbids) in the interests of good training, there's nothing to stop you.

A useful piece of fitness training I have used sometimes when working towards championships was to carry on after the finish of an arduous club race for another lap or two. That is good preparation, both physically and mentally, for bringing out the best in the latter stages of a tough, normal-length race. A friend with whom you practise can make this extra lap tougher by sailing it too and giving you competition.

Valuable as all this is in making the body competition-ready, it may not be enough in top level dinghy sailing to reach the physical condition required to drive the boat flat out in heavy weather all the way round a full Olympic course. For those whose competitive aspirations require them to do that, other methods must also be used. Club sailors who manage only occasional races also need other activities to keep the body in reasonable racing trim.

Running

The body's powerhouse is the heart/lung machine and regular running or cycling are the most convenient ways of exercising the heart and lungs.

A well developed heart/lung machine gives the body greater staying power and greater powers of recovery after a bout of particularly heavy exercise. Some sailors, especially younger ones, will find that their standard, untuned heart/lung machine will get them by for normal club racing, although all will find an all-round benefit in body tone, heavy weather ability and health from some regular exercise other than sailing. Those competing at national or international events in an athletic class must give their internal engine the tune-up that regular running provides if they are to have any hope of success.

For those who don't care for running, cycling or arduous swimming will do equally well. All a sailor should be seeking is to get his heart/lung machine into adequate shape to provide all the power his body needs for two full heavy weather Olympic courses in one day. Any more than that is wasted effort. A two mile run every second day which includes several bursts of hard running, interspersed with very low, loose jogging to relax the muscles, will exercise the heart/lung muscles sufficiently for most sailing purposes. The way you can tell when you're doing enough is that towards the end of long races you're not out of breath, even though you may be feeling the strain in other ways. If you are out of breath the engine needs to be worked on.

Physically the main gain from running and jogging is a boost to the engine's ccs – you become a GT sailor. Some toning up of the body also happens, and with that a general feeling of alertness and well being, both of which are worth having for their own sakes, regardless of whether physical fitness is an immediate priority in your self-coaching or not. But never get sidetracked into excessive physical exercising – that's like putting a Ferrari engine in a Mini.

Now for what running does not do: it does not produce much improvement in the muscles required for sitting out, working the mainsheet, tacking or anything else that you do in a boat. To develop sailing muscles you must either sail a lot or do exercises which particularly work on these muscles.

Gymnastic exercises

Gymnastic exercises are available for developing any set or sets of muscles you need to work for strength, stamina or both. If you need to go to these lengths, go to a good professional coach at a gymnasium and have him help decide which muscles need to be worked on and how. He need know nothing about sailing initially; all he will do is either watch some heavy weather sailing or have it thoroughly described to him using photographs. If he knows his job he will be able to prescribe a set of exercises which work in the desired way on all the main muscles used during a race. Of course he won't work on those alone; he will ensure that other muscles are strengthened up so no physical imbalances develop.

Trapeze crews and helmsmen will necessarily have different sets of exercises. It would be a waste of effort, for example, for a trapeze crew to spend time on a sitting out bench. Why waste time and effort developing physical abilities that aren't needed? There's enough work to do on the abilities you do need without that.

The sailors whose physical needs are for circuit training in a gymnasium are a very small minority of competitive sailors – the other methods of getting fit are much more suitable for most – so I am not going to give a sample circuit training routine for sailors. There are a few points which should be mentioned though. Before anyone starts heavy training of this sort he should have a medical check-up. Any circuit training session should always start with a warm-up period and end with a cooling down period of light exercising. Beware too of getting into a physical fitness ego trip – one ego trip at a time is quite enough. The symptoms are an excessive interest in pulse recovery rates, running speeds and prowess in certain exercises. They can also be directly related to the sailing, for example a crew who is training excessively so he can gybe a 470 with only one hand on the pole in force six. At most that might gain a couple of lengths but only in force six which is little gain to show for weeks of building up arm muscles. Physical training experts always overemphasize the importance of fitness (just as many sailors underestimate it) so don't be tempted into the kind of weight training that might be suitable for a boxer. There have been occasions at the starts of European championships where that training might have been useful, but not normally.

At a physical training session for the British Finn sailors heart recovery rates were being measured and one of the sailors saw that Chris Law's recovery rate was appreciably worse than his own, after which he concluded that heart recovery rate wasn't very relevant to winning Finn races. Nevertheless it has some importance and Chris might have won the Finn Gold Cup by a bigger margin if he'd had that extra fitness.

For the club sailor one gymnastic exercise which he can do at home and which will help his performance is to do sitting out practice. A sitting out bench is easily made in wood. In the first week or two typical daily exercises might be: *Sit out horizontal with the back straight and hold for a few seconds. Pull up so the back is vertical and rest for a few seconds. Return to the sitting out position. Repeat twenty times.* Done every day this will strengthen the sitting out muscles. When it feels fine to do more, speed the exercises up and include some additional ones. When coming in reach right forward to touch your toes. After that add on some exercises to increase sideways mobility: sit out well to the right and when coming in touch the left toes with the right hand. Repeat that ten times. Do the same to the left, touching the right toes with the left hand. Later on longer sequences can be included, with several periods of 30 seconds or a minute of static, horizontal sitting out. The daily routine can be altered, but be careful about over-doing it.

Other, more general toning up exercises, which do not need special equipment are useful for providing a reasonable background of physical fitness. These may be done when a sailor does no other special exercises or running and can be taken from any popular book on getting fit. About ten minutes of exercises a day can make a great difference to general fitness, a difference that those who normally get little exercise will really feel.

Dancing

When John Bertrand stopped for six months and thought about how he was going to reach the top of the world Laser fleet he came to a very interesting conclusion about physical fitness training. What activity, he asked himself, would provide the best all round physical training for Laser sailing? The answer he came up with was modern dance; it is vigorous and exhausting, uses every muscle in the body and the movements are rhythmic, just as movements are when sailing. So he began taking lessons and claims that dancing, combined with regular running and sailing, is the ideal fitness training. Certainly his results in the Laser, the most physically demanding of all classes, do nothing to contradict that.

Yoga exercises

The value of yoga for sailing is only beginning to be recognized, and some leading helmsmen have now turned to yoga exercises to tone up their bodies (and their minds, for that is an important part of yoga) for top level competition. A group of Dutch Laser sailors who trained together and produced the 1979 European champion included yoga in their training. The benefits are greater mobility and smoothness of movement about the boat, greater sensitivity to every movement of the hull through the water and better sense of balance. Yoga also brings more calmness of mind when practised regularly and an all-round toning up of the body.

All this can be gained by doing quite straightforward exercises without any of the headstands or contortions that the advanced yoga students do. The best way to learn is to go to a yoga teacher. If that is not possible there are books explaining the different positions, but the problem with a book is that it can't bend you into the right shape when you are getting it wrong. To gain as much benefit as any sailor will normally need, it is necessary to do about twenty minutes of exercises at least every second day, but ideally every day.

Considerable extra benefits come if, while doing the exercises, the awareness of the reason for doing the exercises is in the back of the mind. This is achieved by bringing your awareness to the boat, the water and fresh air from time to time. The yoga then also becomes a practice for focusing the mind and increasing powers of concentration. Running too can be used in the same way for focusing the mind. Rodney Pattisson says that his daily runs before big competitions are primarily to help him concentrate his mind. But that won't happen unless you decide that it is going to happen, either in yoga or in running. Nor will it happen in a couple of weeks – it may take a whole season before the benefit is fully felt.

There is no need to make a big willed effort; it's more an occasional turning of the attention to the reason for doing the activity, a constant returning in your mind to sailing while doing your exercises. That awareness alone, over a period of weeks and months, is enough to begin to expand your awareness, to focus the mind better and so increase your powers of concentration. But the attention should never be riveted on the subject, it should be brought there in a relaxed and natural way. It will stray off. Fine; that's inevitable and quite natural. After a while it can be brought gently back again, perhaps in total three or four times during yoga exercises or on a run, maybe more. It is very individual and there are no rules, except to do what feels natural, without any mental straining.

Other sports

There seems to be a popularly held belief that for any physical training to be worthwhile it must hurt. Other sports, being enjoyable, therefore don't count for anything with 'serious' fitness addicts. That of course is nonsense. Squash, swimming, skiing, football and tennis all increase general fitness. Played hard they keep the heart/lung machine in reasonable shape and jerk into vigorous action many a muscle that was previously enjoying a quiet life.

Squash is particularly good because as well as being exhausting it places great emphasis on agility and balance. Two hard games a week provide as much general fitness training as any sailor other than those attempting the highest honours requires. Combine this with some static sitting out exercises for helmsmen and perhaps some yoga, and in most classes that will equip a helmsman's body for national level competition. Even one hard game of squash a week provides a considerable boost to the fitness of someone who is otherwise fairly inactive, and it can be a very easy way to keep up a little of the summer's fitness level when not sailing during the winter.

Skiing also gives good exercise for sailors, particularly cross-country skiing. It develops balance and co-ordination, both of which play an important part in sailing. Interestingly, skateboarding can bring spectacular improvement in heavy weather ability. A 16-year-old Mirror sailor who normally finished half to two thirds of the way down his club fleet at Ballyholm in Northern Ireland, stopped sailing completely for several months and went skateboarding when the craze was at its height. When he resumed racing the Mirror at his club, to everyone's astonishment he won whenever it was heavy weather. Somehow skateboarding had given this young helmsman whatever it was that he had previously lacked in physical and mental qualities – certainly actual sailing skills had not been developed as they had been neglected for months. Balance, which is so important in any wind strength, was obviously something that developed as he terrorized the pavements. Perhaps more importantly, he was hungry for the same kind of excitement in his sailing as he'd found in skateboarding; and an aggressive, risk-taking assault on heavy weather is exactly what wins those races.

Windsurfing isn't quite another sport, but nearly. It certainly shows any sailor who has never tried it a vast amount he didn't know about sailing. The body, too, must become more responsive to waves and wind. Balance and feel develop, though it may take several months of regular windsurfing before this heightened sense of balance and bodily awareness develop sufficiently to make a significant difference to a helmsman's ability. But a trapeze crew will feel more immediate benefits.

Surfing is interesting. The main benefit seems to be in the downwind speed ex-surfers have on the sea when they take up windsurfing. This is noticeable because a good number of surfers have taken up the sport. Similar benefits, though probably less obvious, will accompany any surfer who starts to sail dinghies or offshore yachts. Waves are waves, whatever we use to ride them.

Diet

This is a subject in which the number of theories bears a striking correlation to the number of experts. Leading sailors' diets are sufficiently varied for us to say that it's possible to get away with eating most foods just so long as the body is fairly well stoked up. One Laser sailor said he was worried about diet until he went to a regatta at which Bertrand's staple diet was hamburgers. No doubt it would be possible to eat cardboard and win, but we don't have to, not if there's better food to eat.

The most important thing is to eat well and to eat plenty of carbohydrates – bread and potatoes. A good balance of protein is necessary but too much meat has a dulling effect on the body and the senses. Generally sailors do not eat enough fresh fruit and vegetables. Fluid intake is important before and during races, since you lose several pints of fluid during a tough heavy weather race.

So many and varied are the methods of providing ourselves with bodies better equipped to do what we want them to do during a race that you may feel the whole subject is better left alone. Yet it would be a mistake to dismiss this whole area. Equally it would be a mistake to get over-excited about it. There's a balance, a middle road, which is right for each person, and that person himself is the only one to know just what that is. But never think of fitness training as a chore; it is actually an enriching experience which each of us can make more so by choosing those games or exercises which appeal to us. A fit body doesn't in itself produce a fit mind, but it does help. One thing a fit body certainly does produce is better heavy weather racing.

14 Mental fitness

Whatever your present standard, your inherent sailing ability does not vary much from one week to the next, or for that matter, from one part of a race to another. In time, if you work at your sailing, you get better at it; if you don't put some effort in you stay where you are or get worse. But your performance from one race to another, even in similar wind strengths, can be very variable. So what changes?

The big variable is your state of mind. Big differences in performance during a race or a series are because you sometimes draw on your sailing skills in the most productive way, and at other times you don't. Mental fitness is about acquiring a state of mind in which you draw on those sailing skills in the most effective way: more effectively even than on good days before doing any special mental training.

The power of the mind

The wonderful thing about your mind is that provided you go about things in the right way it will do a vast amount for you without your even having to think about it. It does this all the time with mundane

activities like walking and driving the car. This is taken for granted. If your subconscious mind went on strike you would be in dire trouble. Every movement of every muscle would have to be consciously thought out and supervised. You would be a long time getting anywhere.

Your subconscious mind is 90 per cent of the whole, with only 10 per cent representing the conscious part. Just as walking is done almost entirely by the subconscious, so is sailing, much more so than you think. Your conscious mind is simply incapable of attending to every little movement of your body or tuning in to each of the senses which is providing you with the information that is being drawn on. Even tactical decisions are based largely on the subconscious. A situation develops ahead and you need to make a response, and that response, whether to tack or luff or whatever, results from dipping into your store of experience which lies in the subconscious and getting a quick answer. To think through the alternative moves at the time would usually be disastrous.

There is so much to attend to during a race that quite often you have to put your sailing of the boat into automatic pilot while you look for the weather mark, see what the other boats are doing or scan the water upwind for gusts. When you do this you shift your conscious attention entirely off the sailing of the boat, which is done subconsciously by your automatic pilot skills. Only if something goes wrong like a wave taken badly or a sudden heel does a mental alarm bell call your full attention back to the job of sailing the boat.

Even when you are sailing with your attention and thoughts all centred on getting the boat to go through the water as fast as she will, much of your bodily movements and responses are bypassing the conscious mind completely. We are automatons of our own making, and part of making your mind work more effectively on the water is raising these automatic pilot skills – that part which the subconscious mind does for you – to as near perfection as possible.

When your automatic pilot skills are highly developed you automatically sail your boat near-perfectly the whole time. The conscious mind is then free to attend to the tactical side of the race, looking out for windshifts and generally being master of the proceedings and not merely a slavish servant to the jib luff. Much of the time will certainly be spent with full attention on the jib or the waves ahead of the bow or wherever a particular helmsman looks in the prevailing conditions to enable him to get most speed out of his boat.

But little will be lost when he must look away and, all else being equal, it is his studying of the wind and the race as it develops that will enable him to make the winning tactical decisions.

Beginners have no automatic pilot sailing skills; they have to do everything consciously, and even heading up and bearing away have to be thought out. Improvement is a process in which the subconscious learns set responses which allow helming to become a natural, easy and very automatic process. Once your responses do become automatic in this way you face a problem: if these responses are only 70 per cent perfect and you want to improve your racing, you must make the effort to take these automatic skills out, examine them and raise them to a higher level of perfection. That is how you improve.

Re-programming your subconscious, or allowing it to re-programme itself, is obviously a less efficient way of preparing the mind than acquiring a much higher level of perfection in these more basic sailing skills before moving on to develop other skills. This is why I have stressed all the time the need to look for perfection in even the smallest details, for in that way your conditioning of the subconscious is more nearly perfect.

Attitudes within the sport towards mental fitness are very similar to those associated with physical fitness fifty years ago. The idea then was that you got as fit as you needed to be for your sport simply by doing it: no special exercises, no heavy training programme, no special diets. As competition became tougher some top level competitors and their coaches realized that just doing the sport in itself wasn't enough, so special exercises and training methods were introduced which would prepare the body far better for the tasks it faced during competition. Rigorous physical training by top level sailors is now normal and it is spreading back down the fleet.

But when it comes to mental preparation we are back in the 1930s. Most people still have the idea that to equip yourself mentally for top level competition, all you need do is just keep on racing at the top level. But those who are failing to win at the top level, in sailing no less than in other sports, are often failing because they have not equipped themselves mentally to win. At the 1976 Olympics, team managers were insistent that rather than team doctors what they needed were psychiatrists, for it was on the mental side that their sailors were failing.

So the next important development in racing is not going to be in designs nor in physical training methods; it will be in the acquisition of mental fitness. Sailors who want to produce their best when it matters will be as interested in their mental preparation as at present they are in their physical.

What you are looking for are methods of identifying beneficial, race-winning mental attitudes and states and reinforcing them, while at the same time being able to recognize those psychological blocks which deprive you of your best performance and remove them. If you can do both of these things, good days will be even better and bad days will be nothing like so bad. Our good days will be better because your mental preparation will equip you with greater powers of concentration and it will strengthen your will to win, yet you will retain a relatively calm, alert state in which you are not troubled by undue nervousness or anxiety. Nor will setbacks and problems which always crop up during a race disturb your rhythm; it will be possible to dismiss a disastrous start or bad spinnaker drop immediately afterwards and settle back into the groove, sailing to the limit of your ability. This can be achieved by real concentration.

Concentration

Concentration is the one ability above all others that top helmsmen will tell you is absolutely crucial. True concentration is complete absorption of the mind, body and all the senses. It is not just a conscious tuning in on an activity but a linking up at the subconscious level of senses and responses so that by your conscious effort you turn on your whole natural sailing ability – mental, intuitive, physical, intellectual, conscious and subconscious. True concentration does not come through straining or striving but is a one-pointed focusing of the mind in which there is also expanded awareness.

The extent to which the mind must be engrossed in a race to achieve ultimate performance is difficult to describe to anyone who has not experienced the total absorption, the change in awareness and heightened mental powers which true concentration brings. In every moment, with every wave, with every tiny shift of wind there is an opportunity to reach that level of perfection which is an experience in itself and makes gaining on everyone in the fleet inevitable.

All the senses are involved. Sight obviously, but also feel, the sense of touch, balance (most important) and hearing. Because much of this concentration is happening beneath the surface, subconsciously, you don't even know it's happening. But the more the whole of you, all your senses and awareness, can become absorbed in racing, the easier and more intense concentration becomes. Then you no longer need to perform some mental activity called concentrating, you're already doing it.

Considerable improvement in racing ability can come through increasing the powers of concentration. Nick Martin, probably the finest team racing helmsmen Britain has produced and a top 470 sailor, achieves his maximum windward speed by watching the water ahead of his boat and keeping his mind on the *idea* of boat speed. He doesn't know exactly what this does to the way he sails the boat, but he does know that if he shifts his attention away from the idea of boat speed to tactics, or anything else, the boat loses its edge of speed – even though he is still looking at the same area of water and not consciously doing anything different. The thought 'boat speed' activates certain perceptions and intuitive responses and raises them to a higher level which brings his windward sailing to its highest peak.

On the other hand, no matter how intensely conscious attention is focused, your power of concentration can be seriously impaired when one of the other senses is blocked – even if you are unaware that you were using that sense. At the 1976 British Olympic trials Julian Brooke-Houghton, Rodney Pattisson's crew, was complaining forcibly about a small outboard rubber boat which followed *Superdoso* the full length of a spinnaker reaching leg. His complaint was not that the rudder wash disturbed them or that their wind was affected; it was that the outboard was making too much noise to enable him to work the spinnaker properly. The sound that was essential to Brooke-Houghton's handling of the spinnaker was not the crackling of sailcloth but the rushing of *Superdoso*'s bow wave. His eyes were occupied wholly in watching the spinnaker so he could not look at each wave to pick the right moment to sheet in each time *Superdoso* surged forward down the face; instead he picked his moment by listening for the change in sound of the bow wave. No doubt also he would feel the movement of the boat through his umbilical cord of trapeze wire and his legs. But when the outboard engine drowned the crucial sound of the bow wave the natural rhythm of his spinnaker work broke down.

Absorption in sailing with all the senses to this extent is something that happens without you necessarily knowing it is happening. Some top level helmsmen who win races are often unable to say in detail how they do it, yet you have only to watch them sailing their boats to see the intense involvement in the tiniest detail of their every moment.

Before concentration itself becomes a habit – and sometimes afterwards – you may find yourself sailing below your best because your mind is just not on the job and say to yourself, 'Come on, concentrate.' Here you fall into a trap. Instead of concentrating your attention on those things which will produce greater speed or help tactically, you are concentrating on concentrating.

With great resolve you stand over yourself like a schoolmaster over a naughty pupil. Yet with a little less anger and more analysis of the problem you might have noticed that your slow speed was due to the mainsail being sheeted too close to the centreline, the jib fairleads being wrongly set for the wind strength or twenty other details that might account for poor performance. You were forcing your attention to the wrong place.

Concentration induced by a kind of police action of will is second rate for another reason. This forcing of attention to one place by a strong act of will disrupts some of the involvement which is happening at the subconscious level. Bodily and mental tensions are produced which block off some of the flow of communication between the mind, the boat and the environment, reducing your powers of concentration. In true concentration there is also relaxation.

The way to get concentration back when you have lost it is to return to a state of mind in which that essential subconscious flow is no longer blocked by frustration and tension. Our minds are far more powerful than we realize. True concentration focuses our mental energies and we become far more capable. Far from encouraging the development of this one-pointed centring of the mind, the world around us pulls the attention in so many different directions dissipating our mental energies. When we bring all those energies into finer focus and turn them all in one direction we can excel ourselves. Then we begin to realize some of the greater potential our minds possess.

The processes of acquiring this more positive and assured mental state are three-fold, and in the next three chapters, they will be dealt with in greater detail. First, it is vital to recognize and break through the psychological barriers that may be impeding progress. The negative attitudes and beliefs about your ability to win and your will to win itself. This is dealt with in Chapter 15.

In the short term problems may be dealt with as they arise; Chapter 16 gives some first aid treatment. When things are going wrong and threaten to go from bad to worse, bringing on one of those spells where nothing seems to go right, certain mental techniques can be used to put things right and prevent that all too familiar chain of events where one disaster leads to another. These techniques will enable you to put yourself back into top gear again quickly and get on with sailing to the best of your ability. They can also be used to help to get rid of excessive nerves or apathy and establish a good, positive attitude before the race even begins.

The approach in Chapter 17 is longer term. Here we use a method by which the mind can acquire greater powers of concentration, greater calmness under the psychological pressures of important races and through which you are able to draw on your sailing skills and techniques to the full more certainly and consistently than at present.

The biggest difficulty faced when dealing with your mind is that you are dealing with yourself: the work is inward, not outward as sailing technique is. Let's not exaggerate this, though. Learning tactics is also to some extent inward learning. You condition your mind to react in a particular way and, while learning tactics, you recognize wrong ways of acting and modify them so these won't recur. In other words you condition your mind to react in a particular way, which is exactly what mental preparation is about.

15 Psychological barriers to winning

Beliefs and attitudes play an important part in the working of the mind and, in turn, on performance. The more deeply held the belief, the more powerful the effect on the whole of the mind. If you really believe you can win, see yourself as a winner through and through, you will win. This belief will greatly speed up progress in learning to win because you won't rest until you are winning. The opposite belief – that you aren't really all that good – will block your progress, even if you are working at your sailing quite hard and acquiring the skills to do much better.

By analysing your attitudes to a race in the way I am going to suggest, you may find that certain of your mental attitudes which actually prevent you from winning – or at least doing better – can be eliminated, while those that help you to do well can be reinforced.

Pecking orders

Attitudes, like our racing skills, can be acquired by means which almost entirely bypass the conscious mind. These attitudes can damage your performance seriously without your even knowing what is happening. Nor is this something unusual. It happens to everyone, at every level and in every racing fleet.

In the 1976 British Olympic 470 trials Dave White, a sailor who had not previously excelled in the class and had been crewing all the previous year, was lent a boat at the last minute. Against so many top helmsmen he didn't rate his chances too high, but if the races had finished at the beginning of the final beat each day he would have been runner-up. As it was he finished seventh because he lost several places on every last beat. He felt he was doing nothing different on these last beats, but he lost places on them every day. What pulled him back was the belief that he just shouldn't have been up there and that badly affected the way he sailed those final beats.

When people habitually race against each other hierarchies develop. Not the social hierarchies that are a shorebound part of every club, but competitive hierarchies – fleet pecking orders, if you like. For example, if you were given a list of the helmsmen you race against in your club you could probably list an approximate order in which you would expect them to finish in a particular wind strength. And your order would not be very different from the order other people would write down if they were asked to.

I know no-one works out expected finishing orders as a formal exercise, but they do construct exactly such a list in their heads. What's more each helmsman mentally places himself somewhere in that order. When he finishes above his pecking order place he reckons he's done well; when below, badly.

This hierarchy, or pecking order, in a fleet is actually a powerful force, and although I've never seen it referred to before explicitly, it has a much greater effect on actual results than you might suspect. Its effect generally is to restrain change. If you are at the top of the hierarchy, therefore, it serves you well and you should work to preserve it. Most top helmsmen do that in many ways, both consciously and unconsciously. If you are down the hierarchy so that no-one, yourself included, expects you to be at the front of a fleet, then it is very strongly in your interests to break down or change the hierarchy – that is, to change upwards your own and everyone else's expectation of where you will finish.

The realization of just how subservient people are to an accepted pecking order in a fleet came to me when I was crewing some years ago. The lady I was crewing usually finished towards the back of her club fleet. Partly as a result of what I was telling her to do we rounded the first mark third in a twenty-strong fleet. This position was much higher than the others would have expected but, more important, it was much higher than she expected. The result was that when we started on the next leg she looked back in amazed delight at her unexpectedly high position. She was already assessing which boats would overtake us before the end of the race. It was only when I noticed that the boat was no longer being properly sailed that I realized what was going on. She had so upset the accepted hierarchy on this first beat that her day was already made; she had no need to rub their noses in the dirt and was now preparing to drop gently down the fleet towards her accustomed position and be congratulated later for a spectacular first beat.

To retain her position or improve it, would have produced considerable hostility. Result? She had unconsciously decided that the success already achieved was good enough and that the unpleasant reactions to be expected if she completely upset the hierarchy by staying at the front were to be avoided. This unconscious decision hadn't just taken the edge off her sailing, it had slowed us down to the speed of a tail-ender.

When I asked her what the hell was going on and why wasn't she trying to overtake the boat ahead she was genuinely surprised. The thought of *gaining* places hadn't even occurred. Once it had, we went through into second place and then into the lead, winning by 200 yards. The hierarchy had been shattered, because in spite of my being in the boat everyone knew perfectly well that my friend had done all the helming, including working the mainsheet. I had touched only the jib sheets and spinnaker.

It was interesting that in the following races without me as crew her results became spectacularly better than they had been before, although over a period of weeks they trailed off nearer to their earlier level. Certainly I had given practical advice and new knowledge of tactics that was used to improve results in later races but, just as important, I had sharply raised her own expectation of her potential. Her view of her own position in the hierarchy was now much nearer first place.

I make no secret of my own use of this hierarchy concept in winning races. If someone expects you to beat them and you're just astern, the business of overtaking them is made very much easier.

Either they make it easy by not trying, or they make it easy by trying so desperately hard that they upset the natural rhythm of their sailing and make errors. There are countless examples in my own experience of people handing me first place in races in both these ways. And of course as long as they keep doing so, the hierarchical order of things is retained and they secretly expect that next time too they will again be out-manoeuvred and out-sailed. Once you do get past them they usually tend to give up the fight and make only half-hearted efforts to regain their place.

Psyching people out is nothing more or less than a means of altering the hierarchy or, if you're at the top already, reinforcing it. The ritual that many people go through of rubbing down, smoothing, washing and polishing the bottoms of their boats has an almost negligible effect on hull resistance. Its real purpose is to psyche up the polisher and, he hopes, psyche out everybody else.

When an established racing hierarchy is sharply threatened, though, the reaction of those already at the top can be very nasty.

My own worst experience of upsetting hierarchies came halfway through my first season's racing on returning home after three years at university. I set off with a run of first places at my club which shattered the previous season's pecking order. After the first couple of races I was generally being congratulated. After the fifth I was aware of a good deal of, to put it mildly, coolness. After the seventh I discovered that all my results had been struck off the board and replaced by disqualification points. Naturally interested in this new turn of events I asked what was going on. 'Your boat hasn't been measured,' I was told. 'That's because the club measurer didn't keep an appointment we made,' I replied. 'Well you haven't got a proper certificate so you're out.' Which I was. But, interestingly enough, others without proper certificates were not disqualified until I lodged protests to ensure they were.

My crime was not that of sailing with an unmeasured boat (it measured without any problem when checked) but to shatter the existing competitive hierarchy. Having gained their pound of flesh everyone happily accepted my position at the top of the hierarchy for the following season.

Both these are extreme examples of unusually vicious reaction to change in competitive hierarchies, but it is important to realize that any significant change you make in the hierarchy by improving your performance is bound to be met with some kind of resistance. This resistance should be recognized and dismissed for what it is – an unspoken conspiracy by those higher in the pecking order to discourage you from climbing up.

The will to win

People who do really well in races all have a very strong will to win. It is this will to win that enables the aspiring champion to keep searching for improvement all the time, going to open meetings, getting out on the water to practise, taking time and trouble to study sail shapes and examine the champion's boat to see whether there is anything he can learn from that to apply to his own boat.

This will to win by itself will enable an up and coming helmsman to break through competitive hierarchies and develop his skills to a high enough level to fulfil his desire for success. Not all, though, have this burning desire to be top dog, but all have some desire to do the sport at least a little better than they are doing at the moment. So what do you do if your motivation, your will to win, is lacking? Does that mean substantial improvement won't be possible?

To answer this question it is necessary to examine the nature of this will to win. There are two sides to it: one is a desire to prove yourself better than everyone else, the other a deep desire which is in all of us for perfection – in this case perfection in the sport. Now psychologists might analyse the first of these two as a psychological problem which was being sublimated by success on the water. The second is a deep inner need to reach some sort of perfection and can be just as important a part of the will to win as the psychological one. Most people prefer not to analyse their reasons for needing to win since they are only able to recognize in themselves that sense of inferiority which pushes them to prove themselves by success on the water. But when you realize that this is only part of the story you need have no worries about examining motivation.

Too much emphasis on the ego desire for supremacy, in other words bolstering the desire for success by thinking all the time of the club championship or even the gold medal to be won, can actually damage a sailor's chances of gaining that success. Too much emphasis on the goal prevents those subtle yet all-important automatic pilot responses from working properly.

Psychologists have studied this phenomenon of performance becoming worse when motivation is too powerful and their findings are embodied in the Yerkes Dobson Law, which is in two parts. The first part says that performance improves with increased motivation, but only up to a certain point. Then greater motivation actually diminishes performance. The secret of motivation is therefore to keep it at an optimum point. The second part is that optimum motivation is not fixed for an individual but varies according to the difficulty of the skill. The higher the level of skill, the lower the optimum level of motivation. Running and swimming need high motivation while sailing is a low motivation sport because of its high level of skill.

Psyching yourself up for weeks and months before a big event can therefore be a mistake since you may end up over-motivated and so perform worse than usual on the big day. This is exactly why some of the supposedly best-prepared sailors at the 1976 Olympics failed: they were over-motivated. It is also why people go to the big event, do really badly, then a couple of weekends later go to some lesser event which nevertheless contains some top competition and win easily. Building up the ego desire to win, the need to prove yourself better than others, is not therefore in sailing a good tack to take. You don't just have Yerkes Dobson's word for it either. Many sailors have had the experience of sailing worse than usual when it really mattered and when they had really built themselves up to do well, not just once but often.

What happens when you bolster your ego desire to win is that at the same time you are building up your potential fear of losing. And it is this fear which really upsets the subconscious applecart when things start to go wrong. As the desired goal, for which an artificially big need has been built up, threatens to elude you – let's say because you have sailed a bad first beat – the fear of losing begins to seriously affect you. The adrenalin that this releases is no use to you and nor is the mental tension which blocks off some of that subconscious concentration we discussed earlier. As a result you sail even worse.

Building up motivation based on fear is a very negative approach and one I would never recommend. Many have done this, which is why so many people are prepared to win at any price, at the expense of honesty and even enjoyment. No, there is another, positive way.

Instead of emphasizing the rewards and making that your motivating force, your will to win can be strengthened at the deeper level through that desire to find perfection. I don't mean that you should no longer care whether you win or lose, of course you should, just that you should shift your emphasis in preparation and racing from the winning to the perfecting of techniques and skills. By making this shift in emphasis you have no need to artificially boost your will to win, for it becomes more deeply and securely rooted.

Ego desire can then be used positively to build up such sailing skill that considerable improvement and winning become inevitable. Use that natural and entirely healthy desire to win to open up greater perfection in yourself through the way you sail. Show total and complete determination, never give up and that perseverance will develop a rare quality which will produce success, if not now, in the future.

16 Making the least of crises

By using the self-coaching method on all the practical sides of your racing it is possible to recognize weaknesses and find ways of eliminating them which would be impossible with a less objective, less analytical approach. What is true for improving your tacking is also true in principle with your mental attitude, only now, instead of wrong ways of moving, what we are talking about are wrong ways of thinking, wrong attitudes. These are weaknesses in your mental working which you must set about removing if you want to improve, just as surely as you have to improve your ways of moving across the boat if you want to establish a flawless tacking technique.

The first difficulty to be faced in dealing with negative, performance killing mental attitudes is being able to recognize them. For example a confirmed blamer, a superb exponent of the art of finding fault outside himself will always blame his crew, his boat, the weather or anything else for his losing races rather than himself, where the real fault lies, for it is easier to look outward than inward.

Yet the real competition is within ourselves. Win that and success in the outward one is inevitable.

So when tackling mental attitudes the technique of becoming your own coach becomes even more important, for it gives you the necessary distance from yourself, the objectivity to be able to analyse when you are mentally on a wrong tack during a race, then force yourself to take a different tack next time.

Negative attitudes during a race depress your performance; when things are going badly it's as though there is a cut off from the abilities you have. You can see all too clearly that you are doing things badly but just don't seem able to do anything to make things come right. The harder you try the worse you do and the more frustrated you get.

The reason that your performance will sometimes spiral downwards like this is that, hard as you may try to shake it off, some event has brought a negative, performance-killing attitude to the surface and your whole approach is being dominated by that attitude. The worse you do, the more the negative attitude is being reinforced. For example, after an unfortunate piece of spinnaker work which costs a place, a helmsman may be overwhelmed by feelings of 'My crew has let me down – he's ruined my chances of winning' – which would no doubt be expressed to the crew in more descriptive language.

Two things now happen. First the crew, feeling frustrated anyway at his mistake, is made to feel very inadequate or angry, or both, by the helmsman's verbal assault. This makes his crewing worse. Which in turn confirms the helmsman in his belief that the original snarl-up has cost him the race. The helmsman's anger at this, whatever he may be telling himself about keeping up concentration and so on, will block off much of the natural seat-of-the-pants feel which plays so important a part in sailing. So he will continue to sail below his best and the spinnaker snarl-up will continue to be an ever-present tragedy, which first of all stopped him winning, then put him so far off his stride that he later went on to drop four or five more places.

The helmsman's real problem was not the few lengths lost because of the snarled-up spinnaker; it was the emergence of a strong negative attitude, namely: 'My crew has ruined my chances of winning.' So emotionally charged was this idea that it dominated his sailing for the rest of the race, he became trapped in the past instead of living in the present.

This is just one example, but it is typical of the way in which the delicate mental balance which you must retain may be upset. Helming or crewing perfectly is a very complex activity involving whole minds and bodies. When your mind gets hung up on one recurring, negative idea the whole balance and harmony of your racing is lost.

Destructive attitudes during a race do tend to be particularly powerful because they are charged with emotion, just as in the saga of the snarled-up spinnaker. They are more difficult to recognize than those before the race since while racing you tend to be so involved in the events and emotion of the moment that you don't really recognize that there is a destructive, negative attitude at the root of it all. Yet whenever things go badly wrong there will always be found, if you examine the whole thing as objectively as possible, an underlying negative attitude. Get rid of this negative attitude as fast as possible and replace it by a positive one and you again sail to the limit of your abilities.

The bad patches themselves aren't usually too difficult to recognize. You start losing places and sailing worse than usual, and the more you try to pull yourself together the more you seem stuck with the problem. Many people also feel an overall tensing up and a tight feeling in the pit of the stomach. Knowing you are in one of these bad patches is one thing, but doing something to get out of it is quite another.

So what do you do about it? Well, you have seen that it is the power of the emotion – either anger or anxiety – that keeps the negative attitude dominant and so causes a chain reaction of disaster, so the answer is to get rid of the emotion itself as fast as possible. Which is easy to say but difficult to do: making your rational mind control your emotions always is. But there are quite a number of ways you can help your mind win this battle, and win it quickly.

The secret is to distance yourself from your own frustration or anger when things go wrong. And that means first recognizing and accepting the anger or frustration as something that exists, and not trying to fight it by refusing to acknowledge it at all. Once you have accepted that you are in a bit of an emotional state, you have already begun to distance yourself from that emotion. You can now begin to look at your predicament more objectively and see where the real problem lies.

The problem is not what you see as *the cause* of the anger (the crew's spinnaker muddle), *it is the anger itself.* As soon as you can recognize this you have the best possible incentive for getting un-angry. Recovering your cool then becomes a lot easier to do.

If you can remember to do it, the age old method of counting to ten before doing anything is highly recommended. For someone who automatically gives the crew a good bawling out when he does something wrong, the answer is still to bawl them out. But this time – and this is the important part – he should watch himself doing it. Rather than becoming so involved in his anger that he's blinded by it, he is now aware that he is getting rid of the anger by expressing it. In that way the anger can be got rid of fast.

Some people claim that their anger or frustration dissolves away if they turn their attention to the physical changes that it brings, like the much heavier breathing and great increase in bodily tension, especially in the stomach. Evidently, being aware of these symptoms makes the anger itself drain away. Or, for the particularly imaginative, anger can be thought of as something physical which you can get rid of by throwing it over the side.

By achieving some detachment in one of these ways the anger will be less destructive and shorter-lived, so that proper racing equilibrium is restored and the small error no longer boils up into something big. The mistake that was made is very quickly written off, so that the only loss is the distance thrown away by, say, re-rounding the mark, unsnarling the spinnaker or taking the wrong windshift. Nothing more. You are then bringing things under rational control rather than allowing a disruptive emotion to take over. You act more as you would ideally like to act, not as the circumstances of the moment make you act.

Even so, anger and frustration are powerful emotions and it may take some weeks or months of repeated effort before these emotions can be stopped from surfacing so powerfully that they inhibit your sailing for long periods of a race. But when you can become, at least to some extent, master of your emotions, rather than allowing them to master you, you will sail better and more consistently – especially when under great competitive pressure.

This is exactly the approach that enabled Virginia Wade to win the Wimbledon tennis championship on about her fifteenth attempt. Although she had won virtually every other major championship, the nervous tension of playing for the supreme prize in front of her home crowd had always defeated her. The problems usually started after she had taken the lead. She would lose a point through a loose stroke and get angry with herself, which would lead to more mistakes so that she became so tense she couldn't play her game properly. The difference when she finally won in 1977 was that she had learned how to write off each error before starting the next point – in other words, living in the present and not allowing the past to drag her down.

The moving staircase analogy is useful for helping to deal with crises in a race. Once the disaster has happened you drop down a step or two and however angry or excited you get you're not going to be able to regain the higher step. What must happen is that you settle into your sailing again as quickly as possible so you can remain on the lower step and not fall further, for when you remain on that lower step you can be sure that others ahead of you will drop below you as a matter of course. But staying on that step will be impossible if you are not in the right mental state: alert, sharp-witted and competitive, yet fairly calm.

This ability to resume sailing at 100 per cent efficiency immediately after a crisis can also be developed by practice. The method is to introduce a crisis deliberately during a fairly unimportant race. Starting 15 seconds late is one way to do this. The situation would then be exactly the same as if you had messed up the start and had to recover, although the emotions in the deliberate late start would be different. Even so, after recovering well from the deliberate late start, which is much easier since there are no negative emotions, recovery from the identical situation produced by messing up the start becomes easier. The method can also be used during a race where it has been previously planned by the helmsman and crew that each will make at least one deliberate mistake.

Letting go

Tension, physical and mental, is one of the biggest enemies during a race. When you become too tensed up you start to go slowly. You lose places, which makes you even more tense, and you fight to get yourself and the boat going as you know they should. This bodily and mental tension cuts off the easy flow of natural movement and effortless concentration and the ability to acquire that alert relaxation during a race is very important.

The relaxation isn't a 'couldn't-care-less/competition's not-for-me' attitude; it is a state of alert attention in which just those muscles the body requires are being used, without the jaw muscles tensing up, the hands tightening their grip till the knuckles whiten round the tiller, the back and neck muscles becoming rigid. The mind and body must freely be able to respond to every wave under the hull, each minute change in the wind and cope calmly with all the tactical demands. That's the sort of relaxation you need, a letting go.

Tension builds up when you are trying too hard or are trying in the wrong way. Obviously you have got to try during a race or you won't get anywhere. And on some days you don't do well because you aren't trying. So how do you get over this contradiction: on the one hand trying hard is what makes you tense up in a damaging way, on the other hand you must become relaxed without losing any of that essential competitive edge you need to keep you going really well?

The answer is to recognize the over-tense state when it appears and drop back to an ideal state in which you are poised in a relaxed yet alert way. Some people can make this change at will once they have recognized the over-tense state, but they are very much the exceptions. Usually if you *try* to relax you are simply moving to a subtler kind of battle – you are introducing a new kind of effort to fight the tension. And if you're successful at this, you might by conscious effort remove, temporarily, some of the excess tension.

But if you're too successful you might also remove some of the working muscular tension which you actually need to sail the boat perfectly. What's more, the effects will only be temporary. As soon as the conscious effort to relax is stopped, the process goes into reverse and you tense up again. So what do you do?

The answer is not so much to fight the tension but, as with anger, to let it go. And there are various ways to do this. They generally work on the principle that if you've got a neighbour who is annoying you by playing his stereo too loud you don't angrily bang on his wall. Instead of fighting him and perhaps making him turn his stereo up louder, you first get to know him without giving any hint that his stereo is driving you crazy. Then, a day or two later perhaps, you ask him to play his music more quietly and the chances are that he will – without any fights. That's more or less how we deal with troublesome tension.

One relaxation method, for example, is simply to become aware of the tension, accepting it without fighting it, just recognizing that it is there and is unnecessary. Greater relaxation will often follow merely from having this awareness. But always, the important thing is not to get annoyed because you're tense. That only makes you more tense.

Which brings us to a second way of dealing with the problem. Fighting tension doesn't work, so do the opposite – make yourself more tense. If the arms and neck are tensing up, then really tense them up, clench your hands in a vice-like grip round the tiller, tense everything. Hold it for a few seconds, maybe five, then let go. Repeat that a couple more times and some of the tension will release itself, perhaps for the rest of the race, but more likely until the next crisis. For those whose races are continual crises, other methods may be necessary.

Mental and bodily tension can also be eased away by special breathing exercises, since a series of deep breaths has an automatic calming effect. The exercise works like this: take five or six deep breaths, pausing for a second at the end of each in breath before exhaling. Try it now if you like, just taking a natural breathing rhythm and without either straining or hurrying.

Use of the breathing in this way during a race seems somehow to re-centre you on the essentials of the job in hand and releases some of the pent-up tensions which have accumulated. The rhythm of the breathing should be based on the rhythm which is natural in the resting state. So to establish that, just sit comfortably and take a series of deep breaths as before but this time count 1, 2, 3, 4 on the 'in' breath, 5 on the hold and 6, 7, 8, 9 on the 'out' breath. That gives us a 4:1:4 breathing rhythm. This same timing can be used on the water during a race to help calm the mind and ease bodily tension. When the tension problem gets really out of hand the tensing and letting go exercises can be used first, then the breathing.

One way you naturally get into a more relaxed state for racing is by becoming nervous beforehand, Nervousness so long as it isn't extreme enables you to experience various worries and anxieties before the race. Then once you have crossed the start line and got going,the mind is free of the worst fears about how well or badly you are going to sail, you just sail.

My own experience is that some slight nervousness is a necessary part of any really demanding activity, whether it is sailing an important race or giving a talk to a hundred people. If there's no nervousness beforehand the chances are I'll get nervous while doing the job, which can be disturbing. So some nervousness serves a purpose.

Excessive nerves though do damage performance. These can be dealt with by sparing use of the breathing method, which can also be helpful in calming yourself down before the start or when you have gained the lead and are very nervous about holding onto it. The breathing can also be used occasionally before going onto the water, even the day before if necessary, as a calming device. But its use should always be sparing and never over-done. Humming a tune which has especially peaceful and calm associations for you can work in much the same way, though it is less powerful.

Cutting down on the amount of nervous tension anger or frustration doesn't mean you also have to lose any edge of competitiveness. What you lose is the excessive competitiveness. What you are left with is a much more positive approach to racing, particularly when things are going badly or, for the middle-of-the-fleet man, when things are going so uncommonly well that he finds himself unexpectedly in the lead – first place panic can then be dispelled. Like a good rock climber, he now looks not at the dangers behind but at what lies ahead.

17 Mental preparation

Useful as the emergency techniques described in the last chapter are, what you really want is a state of mind which becomes so established that emergency techniques to correct disruptive mental attitudes and emotions during races are unnecessary, or at least so that a minimum time and effort is spent battling with yourself during a race to acquire the right state of mind. To reach such a state of mind longer term methods are needed. In this chapter I am going to deal with ways in which you can consciously alter the way your mind works.

The difficulty you face when dealing with mental approach is that you are tuning yourself: the work is inside rather than outside. If your crew has an attitude to racing that you dislike, you can change him for one with a better attitude; a negative attitude in a crew is easy to recognize. Your own negative attitudes are much more difficult to spot, and they can't simply be left ashore in exchange for more positive ones.

Or can they? Well, not immediately, but over a period of weeks and perhaps months your own attitudes can be made much more positive. And the more securely positive they are, the better you will sail, even under the most extreme pressure and in all conditions.

Take, for example, a helmsman who always does well in heavy weather but when it drops light finishes nowhere. The helmsman will tend to say things like 'Give me a blow, I'm no good in light stuff.' What's more, he will often give out this kind of statement as pre-race publicity on light air days, so that his imminent bad result is explained away beforehand. Having let everyone, especially himself, know that he is going to do badly, that's exactly how he does. No-one likes to be proved wrong.

What this helmsman is really doing is to opt out of the race before he starts, though he will go through the motions of sailing it. He has become so disillusioned with his light air performance that not only does he see himself as a heavy weather sailor, but in his own mind he only really competes at all in heavy weather. Thus his level of results are (if you don't count the light air races, which he doesn't) quite good.

There are lots of other attitudes people hold which ensure that, under certain conditions or against certain helmsmen, they will not do well. Now the important point here is that the attitude itself is what depresses the performance, for without this negative, losing frame of mind, the helmsman would be able to sail to the limit of his technical racing skill. With his mental block ('I'm no good in light stuff') he sails well below his best, and would still do badly, even with the fastest boat in the fleet.

This is a fairly extreme, though not uncommon, example. To become a good all-round helmsman he must begin by at least modifying his approach to light air competition; it would be too much to expect him to discard his defeatist light air attitude right away. The first thing he should do would be to become interested in light air sailing, while accepting the fact that he couldn't immediately become successful at it. The very fact of studying the art of making boats move well in virtually no wind will focus his attention on his sailing in drifting conditions. And once he has achieved a reasonable level of concentration on the job in hand his performance will show at least some improvement. This improvement is itself encouragement for further effort, which in turn produces further improvement.

In this way his attitude changes by degrees from 'I'm no good in light stuff' through 'I'm going to try and do something about my light air sailing' to 'I'm beginning to understand what these other guys are doing that makes them go so fast in no wind' and eventually to 'I'm getting the hang of what light air sailing's all about.'

The same gradual approach can be used to remove any attitude which prevents you making the most of the sailing abilities you have, or which stands in the way of further improvement. At the same time you can reinforce your positive attitudes.

The heavy weather sailor was doing exactly the right thing to make his heavy weather sailing even better: he was thinking very positively about it, telling himself and everyone else that he was really a heavy weather sailor. So by seeing himself as being good in heavy weather and projecting this image to others around him he became even better. But only in heavy weather. In light air, until he modified his attitude, he was still a washout.

If you are genuinely able to convince yourself that you are especially good in certain conditions (ideally all conditions) or that you sail faster than a certain helmsman, then you do indeed become good in those conditions and will usually outsail the helmsman. And the longer and more deeply a positive belief is held, the greater will be its effect on performance.

Keen teenagers tend to have the most positive attitudes to their racing. Not only do they already have the will to win, but they turn that easily into a working belief that they can win. This is not a belief that they usually keep to themselves but let everyone know who's prepared to listen (and some who aren't). In a very few seasons these helmsmen become as good as they've been telling everyone they were. This seems to quieten them down.

There are of course a vast number of positive and negative attitudes which a helmsman may bring to his sailing, and these will vary from day to day. On a bad day some of the more negative ones will dominate, while on a good day the positive ones take over. For every negative, performance-killing attitude there is always its positive, race-winning counterpart. So having identified a negative attitude of your own, you can then look for the positive attitude that corresponds to it and go onto the water with that in mind, just as your heavy weather expert did. Here are just a few common negative pre-race attitudes together with their positive counterparts:

Negative	*Positive*
Not another flukey day. There's more skill in bingo than this.	A shifting wind. Nice. Let's really get somewhere by reading the shifts right today. I'll go

	out early and sail the first beat to get the rhythm of them.
The boat's slow in this wind we can't expect to do anything.	Elvström could win in this boat just as it is. Let's see how I can do. After the race I'll get someone to help me to sort out the tuning.
It's a flat calm, I might as well not bother.	Lovely, a drifter. A lot of them won't even be trying.
This is going to be my bad day, everything's been going wrong.	Maybe things haven't been going too well, but let's see if we can excel ourselves anyway. Everybody else has bad days, so if it's our turn let's do better on ours than they do on theirs.
etc.	etc.

Yet the same method can be used to remove any other performance-killing attitudes. First recognize the attitude – 'we're too light for this wind strength', 'I never do well in big fleets', and so on – then find the positive attitude which will replace it. Spend a little time thinking about the hopeful, positive side so that you go onto the water without the backward pull of a performance-damaging attitude. A little time is needed for this mental transformation since it's one thing to tell yourself what the right attitude is, but quite another to convince yourself sufficiently to truly acquire the positive, race-winning attitude.

Our heavy weather expert might take the best part of a season before he really enjoyed light air racing, and only when he did would his earlier defeatist approach be completely washed away. But the shift would have begun through the most basic change of all, a change in the way he thought.

The most difficult attitudes to alter are those we attach to helmsmen who nearly always beat us. Because a particularly good helmsman you sail against often beats you, you accept the fact that he is better than you. Yet this acceptance of inferiority is already a negative attitude which will make beating him more difficult. To sail at your best when in close quarters with him you must change your attitude.

But how can you hope to convince yourself that he isn't better than you when the results sheet seems to say quite clearly that he is? To answer that we must analyse very carefully what his superior results really mean. They do not mean that he is better than you; they mean that he is doing the job of winning sailing races better than you are doing it. So tell yourself 'It's not *him* that's better than me; it's simply that what he is doing is being done better than I am doing it *at the moment.*'

By this shift of emphasis you change the attitude from a fixed one, a black and white 'he's better than me' idea, to an attitude which, instead of reinforcing his superiority, opens up for you the idea that you're going to do the job of racing even better than he's doing it, given just a little time. The change in the way of thinking here may seem small, but it can make all the difference.

Changing mental conditioning by repeated use of rational analysis alone is a long term business and you might sometimes feel you are fighting a losing battle. Other methods are available which can help. The East Germans, Russians, Japanese and others use autogenic training, which is one way of willing the mind powerfully to work more as you want it to work.

Autogenics is derived from hypnosis and resembles a form of self-hypnosis, with a difference that whereas hypnosis produces drowsy brain wave patterns, autogenic training produces more vigorous rhythms. The technique is practised alone three times a day for five or ten minutes sitting or lying down.

Assertion, imagination and concentration are used to produce the desired change in mental attitude or physiological response but primarily autogenics is a form of self-programming so that the mind and body will behave more as you want them to and less as they do. For example the technique can be used for reducing excessive nerves without removing the physical and mental ability to give peak performance to produce a more positive mental attitude.

Drugs are often used by sailors to reduce their mental tensions and to enable them to sleep, but other methods should always be used if possible. Sleep induced by drugs is of lower quality than natural sleep. When sleeping we go through various stages, and rapid eye movement sleep which is associated with dreaming is especially important. Deprive people of this and their work performance reduces. Yet almost all drugs affect eye movement sleep, with barbiturates the biggest offenders.

Sailors also calm themselves sometimes by taking tranquillizers. A leading helmsman in the 1976 Olympics took them before most of his races, which was perfectly legitimate since the Olympic organizers have legislated only against drugs which activate the mind, not calm it. Again, though, drugs are a poor substitute for other means of calming the mind because they also dull the senses, which in sailing is definitely not what we want.

Meditation, on the other hand, is an excellent means of bringing calm to the subconscious and acquiring the ability to dive deep down into the mind, not by force but by a natural process. The interesting thing about meditation is that one finds something beyond the subconscious, a deeper dimension: that which Tim Gallwey, in *The Inner Game of Tennis* refers to as Self 2. And this is the perfect automatic pilot, more perfect than can be acquired by conscious conditioning of the subconscious alone, although preparation by practice, observation and racing is of course necessary. Over a period of time it can bring a whole new dimension to sailing. Through regular practice you can open up these more intuitive, deeper levels of the mind which bring you closer to being able to do the right thing spontaneously, bring more calmness of mind, draw on your highest level of ability much more of the time and help you to acquire greater powers of concentration.

By regular practice of the right meditation combined with regular sailing, the unfolding of these qualities happens automatically. You don't need to do any of the practices during the race, just as you don't need to do special physical exercises while sailing. You get physically fit over several months by training ashore and that fitness is there available to you while sailing. It's just like this with meditation and the mind.

18 Preparing for major combat

There are many ways a helmsman can use the period before a race for getting his mind into the ideal state for competing, and at a championship the way the time after a race is spent is important too. How each individual goes about putting himself into the right frame of mind during championship series is up to him and no two people will go about it in exactly the same way, but there are some dos and don'ts which apply generally.

Do be aware that state of mind is important Try to identify anything in the pre-race period, including the night before, which contributes to a race winning frame of mind. This takes time and means including the hours and evening before a race in the post mortem race analysis. It makes a great difference to some people, for example, whether they drive to a championship regatta alone or with others. If it's necessary for you to be alone to give of your best the following day, make sure you do drive alone.

Do use the time of waking up to start the day well Don't leap straight out of bed. Wake up slowly and wake up happy. That is very important. Bring in positive thoughts such as 'I am capable of great things today' – which you are, but you need to remind yourself of the fact, and the moments of waking are an especially good time to do so. Be conscious of the body and how good it feels when you stretch. Relax the body. If you do yoga exercises then do those for ten or twenty minutes. They are beneficial for both body and mind. It is also a good idea to have something inspiring to read which encourages your own belief in yourself. It might be a story of some heroic feat like climbing Everest, a love story, the writings of an Eastern sage or a book on the power of positive thought. What it is doesn't matter, as long as you find it in some way inspiring, the more inspiring the better. Music too can help the day start well, but whatever else you might be first thing in the morning, be happy.

Do think positively about the coming race You are going to do your best, tell yourself. It doesn't even matter if you don't win. Maybe on this day your best isn't good enough to enable you to win. That doesn't matter, just as long as it's your best. Tomorrow, next week, next month, next year your best may be good enough to produce the win. Maybe it is today. But don't get hung up on first place. Your best is what matters, for you can do no better than that. And when you do achieve that an interesting thing starts to happen – your best gets better, automatically.

Do not dwell on past failures When someone has his self-coaching working properly this should not happen, for the coach-self should have assessed those performances, learned from them and given the sailor-self practice procedures and training exercises to cut down the chances of the failures recurring. But some will worry nevertheless, so how do they break out of the downward spiral they are in?

If it is severe and the negative phase has lasted several weeks or even months they probably shouldn't even be at the regatta. There is a golden rule which says if you're not enjoying racing give it a rest for a while. Because if you're not enjoying it you do badly and if you do badly you enjoy it even less and if you enjoy it even less you do worse still and then you disappear down your own bung holes. Then a temporary change of class or scenery is required. But that is for chronic cases.

Mild cases of pessimism will respond to a combination of the remedies suggested in this chapter, plus a deliberate, slight lowering of expectation for yourself. Any place in the first five is better than twentieth. But above all go out to enjoy the sail and do your best, whatever happens. Enjoy the way the hull moves through the water, enjoy the sun (even the rain), enjoy being in a boat, feel lucky to be taking part in such a superb sport. Sing to yourself before the start. And remember, poor past performances are very easy to improve on, so go out and do so.

Do get to the boat park in good time A rush to get afloat leaves no margin for error if some piece of equipment needs attention. Some people find they sail better when the race begins the moment they arrive late at the boat park. I always found myself unusually well attuned to the job of racing if I had to rush to rig and only just made the start line by the 10-minute gun. Partly of course that was to give people the idea that I was very casual about the whole thing (which I wasn't), and that was intensely puzzling to the bottom polishers and dedicated fittings tweakers when they got beaten. It seemed to make the beating of them easier. But that way is fraught with peril and if I were doing any serious racing now I would rid myself of that particular way of getting the mind into top gear. There are many ways it can be done without skimping on proper pre-race practice and assessment of the course. One of these is mental rehearsal.

Do some mental rehearsal Winning, given similar equipment, sailing technique and ability, is in the mind. Using mental imagery on the evening of a race and again the next day helps to bring out the more positive, race-winning sides of ourselves; it increases the odds on doing everything right. In other sports this is a normal part of preparation for top level competition.

Do not be distracted by the psyching out tactics of others Some sailors like to make a point of doing things which upset their closest rivals. It is always worth remembering that their motive is insecurity, however confidently they may do their psyching. They are doing it because they see you as a threat and want to lessen that threat before the start. Do not retaliate. Instead, accept, privately, the psyching attempt for the compliment it is. Then beat them.

Do not deliberately psyche anybody out It always rebounds sooner or later, and against close rivals who have read the previous paragraph, sooner.

In 1976 Rodney Pattisson went to the Olympics with an FD

equipped with the kind of electronic wind speed and direction equipment used on ocean racers. Lightweight equipment of that kind was new at the time and the rest of the FD fleet who didn't have it was thoroughly psyched out, although Rodney unplugged the electrics before every start and sailed the regatta without their help. Effective as this ploy was in undermining the confidence of some sailors who should have known better, Rodney was disqualified in the first race after an incident just after the start with another boat. The two things may well have been unconnected but concerted effort put into psyching others does sometimes rebound unpleasantly in that kind of way. Superior sailing rather than deliberate psyching is the best way to win.

Deliberately psyching out others also ends up more often than not with you psyching out yourself. Sail well enough and they psyche themselves out anyway. Then there is no inner backlash to emerge later and upset one of your future performances.

Do make sure there is nothing to upset your sailing Read the sailing instructions thoroughly so there are no unknowns to worry you when out on the water. Make sure before going to the championship that all your business and family commitments are taken care of so you have no anxieties troubling you during the event, because if you have you'll do badly. The boat too must be right so that you are entirely happy with it, otherwise you may sail below your best. Do whatever is necessary to get the boat completely race-ready.

Do remember the feeling you had before successful races Whatever is conducive to that feeling, do it, for that is the right state of mind for you. Make that feeling an end in itself and avoid doing anything that disturbs it.

Don't indulge in superstition This is something which is rarely spoken of by leading sailors but commonly indulged. A particular piece of clothing, a dressing routine in which the left sock must always go on before the right one, the ritual of boat rigging must without fail be done in a particular way . . . These rituals do serve some purpose: they help the sailor to believe he is attuning himself mentally to the task ahead, and if he believes that some good is done because belief in oneself is essential for success. But they provide a very superficial form of mental preparation and if they are interrupted or cannot be done in the required way for some reason a sailor inevitably feels 'fated' to having a bad day, which, because he believes that, he has.

At one time in my racing I became unduly superstitious. Among my mumbo jumbo items was a sweater which I regarded as lucky and which I had to wear if I was going to win. There were also 'lucky' routines which I made a point of going through before going afloat. This all got rather ridiculous and one day I realized as much and decided to do something about. What I did was to throw away the sweater, which by then was hopelessly tatty, and do no 'lucky' rituals. I not only won the race but more importantly won the battle with superstition and rid myself of the idea that I always had to put the mainsail up before the jib and similar nonsense.

Do eat sensibly Racing makes big demands on the body and unless it is properly fuelled it will not do what is required of it. A depleted body also affects the mind and performance drops off sharply. A good breakfast is essential, as is an energy giving drink taken on the water during championship and other long races.

Don't get drunk Some pretty good sailors I know claim they sail best with a hangover but as I've never seen them race without, comparisons are difficult. Many international sailors, on the other hand, take abstinence to religious extremes. A glass or two of wine or beer in the evening does no harm whatsoever and will actually benefit the more tense competitor by relaxing him. Getting tense is easy; letting go is the hard part, and a little drink can be a great help with that.

Do sleep well This is so obvious that hardly anyone ever talks about it, but the fact is that the front runners at major events often suffer from insomnia; Elvström had done so. Yet lack of sleep is more damaging to our performance than almost anything else. Even a person's routine office work suffers when he hasn't slept well, so how much more must those finely tuned skills of boat handling and racing tactics suffer? That is one reason why someone sails well enough to gain the overall lead in the regatta early on and then fails in the last two or three races. The excitement of success and anticipation of tomorrow's race just don't enable him to sleep properly.

Don't take drugs if they can possibly be avoided. Drug induced sleep is of inferior quality. Dreaming is essential to the equanimity of the mind and sleeping drugs inhibit dreaming. Everyone should find their own way of dealing with insomnia. My own way is to do twenty minutes of yoga exercises either late at night if I feel restless or in the middle of the night. It rarely fails and on the few occasions it doesn't work, the mind and body become much more rested.

Do some exercise after light air races Having exercised over several months to preapre the body for hard physical activity, you must give the body that if the weather doesn't. During a light air series those who have trained to produce good bodily fitness for heavy weather often get tense and edgy after a day or two. They also have trouble sleeping. All this is because the body was being exercised regularly and suddenly is not. A good run after light air races also produces a better night's sleep and therefore better mental and physical state for the next day's racing.

Do not get too excited about winning This will have a bad effect on your next race. It is important to contain your enthusiasm over winning a series race, just as it is a bad mistake to make a big thing of congratulating yourself after a successful first beat. The race is only one of a series, just as the first beat is one leg of a race. We can all take a lesson from Borg here. After winning a set in a Wimbledon final, he allows himself barely a smile, for there is another set to come. But once he has won the final point and the championship he falls to his knees and raises his arms to heaven.

Do not let the press affect you If your past performances are such that you are interesting to the press, do not let their questions unbalance your preparation. For those who the press do interview, give the subject some thought. You cannot improve your chances by what you tell the press; you can only damage them. Saying too much can create big pressures, as Paul Elvström found in 1952 when asked by Danish radio how he would fare. 'Oh, I'm going to win,' he replied. 'I can't see how I can lose,' and promptly regretted it. 'I should never have said that because I got so many naughty letters. And from that time my nerves started. I had no experience, I was only honest. I had worked so hard that I didn't believe anyone could beat me. After that, even if I thought I would win I would never say it. Never. I was only honest in '52 but that was too hard.'

Pattisson refuses to have anything to do with them before and during important events. That policy does create problems, though, because the refusal causes tension. The best policy for most people is to be straightforward and brief, never giving predictions about their likely finishing positions.

In sports which are more televisual and where media pressures are far greater athletes are sometimes schooled by their coaches, who give them mock interviews and provide lists of typical press questions so they are well prepared.

Enjoyment of publicity is something to beware of: it brings a little temporary fame but makes winning, as Elvström discovered, more difficult.

Do enjoy the social side Championships should never be a week-long penance, where all that matters is winning and there is no humour or fun. According to Elvström, 'If you are fair and a nice man to everyone, they will accept that you are first; if you are not, then nobody will accept that you are first. So it is much easier to be first if you are nice.' What about John Bertrand, does he think the social side of a regatta is important? 'Yes I do. Especially at a World Championship. It has to be an event. It can't just be racing. If you do well in a regatta, it is going to be a good thing on top of your success, but for the people who don't do well, you have to give them something, a good memory to take home.'

The other competitors are all your friends – unless you make them otherwise.

Do use that extra something which is available at a big event There is something extra available to draw on during an important race. Focusing on the race during the run-up period also builds up mental energies and concentration. The well prepared sailor, like the concert pianist, uses the extra energies inherent in a big event to rise to greater heights than otherwise he could. Pattisson has done this repeatedly. The less well prepared cannot handle this extra energy; it brings out in them tensions and fears which make them sail worse than usual. How a sailor copes with the biggest challenges is a measure of his mental and physical preparation.

Don't take all this too much to heart These are guidelines, not rules to be slavishly followed, so get out there and sail for all your worth. In the end that's all that counts.

Conclusion

This book is no more than a key. It is up to you whether you use it to unlock the door of your own true sailing abilities – abilities which all have in great abundance, but very few come even close to realizing.

True winning is within ourselves: achieving our best, our finest possible performance given the natural abilities we have. It is not measured by finishing order necessarily. Outwardly we may lose, but within ourselves we have won.

Some of the most memorable races I have ever sailed, I lost. They had everything – excitement, close battles, difficult tactical decisions, total enjoyment, the real thing. Losing did not annul all that nor, as happens when the result is built up to over-blown proportions, did the memory of all that highly competitive racing die. I did all I could that day and somebody just happened to do it better. Bloody inconvenient – but oh what a race!

When winning becomes a religion, first place is all that matters, and losing is a sin against that god of outward success. For adherents to that religion the sin is bad enough; to enjoy it is heresy of the worst kind. Sin must be punished, which these sailors who religiously slave towards success do by mentally chastising themselves and becoming unhappy. You can see them at many of the major events. All this is no fun for those they are sailing against and no fun for them.

Winning should never ever be a religion and true winning can never be, for it is inner winning – your own personal sailing fulfilment, doing the sport as well as you can do it by letting at least some of your inner sailing genius out. That is real winning. The other becomes glory seeking where sailing is merely the vehicle for glory seekers to try and reach their goal. Not that there is anything in the slightest wrong with glory as the deserved reward for true effort, but when the quest for gold denies enjoyment and honesty, and ruins the sport, there is something wrong.

Slavish pursuit of sailing's rewards for their own sake is never going to bring real satisfaction. Fame and respect, locally, nationally or internationally, depending in which league you are – and the tin trophies which are worthless in themselves – are all temporary. Yet when you strive for perfection you find something more permanent. You also find something more immediate – the sheer joy of competitive sailing. When you find that you are really a winner, whatever your present sailing standard. The only difference your level makes is that the higher you go the more of that inner sailing genius you open up in yourself and the more enjoyment that brings. It is the satisfaction, the warm inner glow, of doing something very, very well. First place is a nice pat on the back for doing that, but it isn't absolutely essential.

Photographic acknowledgements and captions

All photographs were taken by Guy Gurney except at Chapter 1, Alastair Black, and at Chapter 9, Malcolm and Frances Donald.

Chapter	Page	
1	1	Eric Twiname on his own International Canoe.
2	6	Flying Dutchman dinghies have difficulty setting spinnakers.
3	12	Solings attack in rough seas.
4	21	Getting an Olympic Finn round the mark.
5	31	British and French competitors learn all about the Three-Quarter Ton Cup.
6	43	Concentration by young Germans aboard a pair of Optimist dinghies.
7	55	A Soling undergoes a vicious broach.
8	69	Port but also starboard gybes by the Olympic 470s on the way to the leeward mark.
9	77	On the way to another win, a one-off One Tonner, *Rakau*.
10	83	Close quarters for a German, a Danish and a Canadian Finn.
11	88	Sailing school practice in 9½ feet Turnabout class cat rigged dinghies at Newport, Rhode Island.

Index